The Way
of the
Lover

About the Author

Ross Heaven is the founder and director of the Four Gates Foundation, one of Europe's leading organizations for the teaching and application of spiritual wisdom and Freedom Psychology™. The Four Gates offers workshops in empowerment, self-awareness, and practical shamanism through trainings that range from weekend events to one-year programs and home-study courses. These include introductions to shamanism and shamanic healing, plant spirit shamanism, the Four Gates to Freedom and Way of the Lover workshops referred to in this book, as well as spiritual initiations, and Darkness Visible®™retreats, which are based on shamanic and spiritual practices in which participants remain in physical darkness for the duration of the five-day course.

Many of these workshops are based on Ross's books, which include *The Journey to You, Spirit in the City, Vodou Shaman, Darkness Visible, Plant Spirit Shamanism, The Spiritual Practices of the Ninja: Mastering the Four Gates to Freedom,* and *Love's Simple Truths: Meditations on Rumi and the Path of the Heart.* His work has been featured in national newspapers, on radio and television, and in films and documentaries.

He has a website at www.thefourgates.com, where you can read more about his books, workshops, and healing practice.

The Way of the Lover

Rumi and the Spiritual Art of Love

Ross Heaven

Llewellyn Publications
Woodbury, Minnesota

FIRST EDITION
First Printing, 2007

Book design by Rebecca Zins
Cover design by Gavin Dayton Duffy
Cover images: PhotoDisc (Rose)
Interior image: Wheel on page 19 from
Art Explosion, ©2004 Nova Development

Library of Congress Cataloging-in-Publication Data

Heaven, Ross.
  The way of the lover : Rumi and the spiritual art of love / Ross Heaven.—1st ed.
      p. cm.
  Includes bibliographical references and index.
  ISBN-13: 978-0-7387-1117-1
  1. Sufism—Doctrines. 2. Spiritual life—Islam. 3. Love—Religious aspects—Islam.
  4. Jalal al-Din Rumi, Maulana, 1207–1273. I. Title.
  BP189.3.H43 2007
  297.4'4—dc22

                                                      2007019769

Llewellyn Publications
A Division of Llewellyn Worldwide, Ltd.
2143 Wooddale Drive, Dept. 978-0-7387-1117-1
Woodbury, MN 55125-2989
www.llewellyn.com

Printed in the United States of America

Contents

The Religion of Love
Introduction by Syed Hamraz Ahsan ... ix

1. **The Masters of Love**
   Stepping Onto the Path with Heart ... 1

   Seekers After Happiness, 4
   Rumi: The Flowering Soul, 8
   The Lover's Wheel: Medicine Teachings, 11
   Merging Forms: A Sufi Medicine Wheel, 16
   The Map of the Journey, 18
   How the Stream Crossed the Desert, 22
   Taking the First Step, 28

2. **The Birth of the Lover**
   Why Our Souls Fear Love and Love Fear ... 29

   The Journey of the Soul, 30
   Where Did I Come From? 33
   Myth-conceptions, 34
   Meetings with God, 35
   Facing Our Fears of Love, 38
   Where All Fears Begin, 40
   Forms of Fear, 42
   The Growth of Fear, 43
   The Mood of the World, 44
   These Fatal Wounds, 46
   Explorations, 50
   How Etsaa Became the Sun, 55

3. **Seeking the Beloved**
Where True Power Can Be Found ... 57

    Powerful Myths, 58

    The Illusion of Power, 59

    Grabbing Power from Others and Losing It for Ourselves:
        Family Scripts and Dramas, 62

    The Shocking Conclusion, 63

    Meditations on Not-Being, 65

    When We Are Not Selfless, 75

    Loving the Tyrant, 77

    Explorations, 81

    The Priest Who Knew Too Little, 84

4. **Life Games and Their Players**
Finding a Pathway to Love ... 85

    The Games of Life, 87

    In the West of the Wheel, 94

    Knowing How to Know Truth, 95

    The God in the Hat, 96

    All That We Know, 98

    Explorations, 100

5. **Staying Awake on the Path**
Avoiding That "Is It All Worth It?" Feeling ... 105

    But If Not Love, Then What? 107

    The Value in Suffering, 109

    Scars, 112

    The Compassionate Soul, 113

    The Beauty of Death, 115

    Living with Patience and Good Intentions, 117

    Nothing Matters, 118

    Explorations, 119

6. The Medicine Wheel of Relationships
Balancing Ourselves & Finding Our Way to the Center ... 127

Balancing the Four Bodies, 128
Harmonizing the Physical Self (The East), 134
Harmonizing the Emotional Self (The South), 136
Harmonizing the Mental Self (The West), 137
Harmonizing the Spiritual Self (The North), 140
Enhancing Mystical Powers (The Center), 141
Explorations, 143

7. Completing the Circle
What Our Relationships Teach Us ... 147

Self-Knowledge: Shrinker of Journeys, 149
The Map of Loving Relationships, 150
The Soul of Souls, 156
Explorations, 157
The Beetle and the Broomstick, 160

8. Strive to Be a Lover
Throw Away the Books & Start a Revolution! ... 161

The Wise King, 163

References and Further Notes, 167
Index of Terms, 181
Index of People and Traditions (by first name), 189
Acknowledgments & Thanks, 193
Disclaimer, 195

The Religion of Love

Syed Hamraz Ahsan

> *I follow the religion of Love;*
>
> *whatever way Love's camels take,*
>
> *that is my religion and my faith.*
>
> IBN AL-'ARABI

ufis are divine lovers, and the great Sufi masters like Ibn al-'Arabi and Rumi are beacons lighting the way for all travelers on the path of love. This path begins at the heart and ends at the heart.

But the ways of God are strange and so are the ways of man (which is only fitting if you consider that Sufis believe man was made in the image of God), and so this pathway to love and the divine may not always be simple or clear.

In the old days, for example, in the city of Gangowah, India, there was a Sufi master called Shaikh Mohammad Sadiq. He had a disciple by the name of Sheikh Jamal who could not concentrate when engaged in Sufi practices. His mind always wandered.

When he was instructed by his shaikh to perform a very difficult Sufi practice in complete isolation for forty days, he hesitantly confessed his problem to his spiritual master. The shaikh asked, "What do you love most in this world?"

The disciple's answer was unusual: "I love my black buffalo with long horns." The master thought for a while and said, "It is fine; this problem can be solved. When you do this practice and invoke the name of God, concentrate solely on your beloved buffalo."

Sheikh Jamal went into a small room and started his practice. After forty days, the door of that small meditation room was opened, and the shaikh called for his disciple to come out. But Sheikh Jamal cried out from inside, "Oh, master, I cannot come out because big horns have grown on my head!" The master then forcefully pulled his disciple out of the small door.

When Sheikh Jamal came out of that meditation room, he was no longer an apprentice but had become a perfect lover. So even the love of a buffalo can bring us to an understanding of God and the divine! For Sufis, everything is an expression of God, including buffalo, and it is no different with love: in love we meet—and become—God.

When the last century was in its sixties, I was in my early twenties: full of energy, enthusiasm, and exuberance. I was also a revolutionary. I fell in love with a married woman, ten years older than me. It was an unrequited love, and I suffered much.

For my revolutionary friends, it was meaningless suffering. To console me in those days, they would frequently recite what was probably Karl Marx's only quotation on love: "If you love someone without evoking love in return and your living expression does not convert yourself into a loving being, then your love is impotent, a misfortune."

But then, and now, I always believed that Karl Marx was wrong on that point. Even one-sided, unproductive love is not a misfortune. It has the potential to produce the most potent love in the world. *Love, in whatever stage, in whatever shape, in whatever disguise, is still love.* As Ross Heaven writes, love is energy—the most powerful energy. It has to go forward, upward, downward, and in all four directions. My love guided me to the Sufi path.

Love is the only theme, the only objective, the only point, the only center, and the only core that all of Sufism revolves around. Extended ritual, great sufferings, mortification, and a warrior-like fight against one's ego are just necessities or inevitabilities on the path to achieve the real goal: true love. The process is itself important, as it makes the lover's soul/spirit pure, reflective, and gracious. The peripheral effects are that those beautiful souls and spirits of the active lovers among us become divine blessings, not only for mankind, but for all organic and nonorganic life in this mysterious cosmos. Their blessing is a continuous process that will stay with us even after our physical departure from this world. Our souls, in their long journeys through many planes, will always find solace in the blissful presence of the pure and kind souls of lovers. Their luminosity provides us with nourishment, which is essential for our souls to breathe and grow.

Without their purity and freshness, their kindness and benevolence, life would be breathless and, to a great extent, worthless. They are a real blessing for us, and we all should be grateful for this divine graciousness.

Among these beautiful souls are ones such as Rumi, who are known by Sufis as *aashiq*: the arch lovers. They practiced love with such vigor, such intensity, that they were totally absorbed in their beloved. They surrendered themselves completely and asked in awe, "Who am I anyway?" They had forgotten whether they were lovers or beloved. All differences, all dichotomies, disappeared as if they were never there. They found "oneness." The perceived separation disappeared and they became God, the divine. Then they declared with exuberance that there is nothing but God.

Somebody once asked a Sufi his name, and the Sufi drowned in his thoughts but could not recall it. All that was there in his memory was his beloved's name; there was nothing else. Another Sufi used to forget which of his legs was right and which was left. He had to wait at the door of the mosque until somebody could tell him. Then, as is stipulated in Islam, he would put his right foot first in the place of prayer. He had reached the stage where sides do not exist. Whichever side the ardent lover looks, he finds only his beloved.

The destiny of every Sufi is merger with the beloved. That state is called *fana fi Allah*, annihilation in God. But that is not the end of the story. They have to return to the mundane world. That is the highest stage in Sufism, called *baqa bil Allah*, subsistence in God. But this time they are not separated from God because there is no lover and no beloved, there is only oneness. Only Love.

From the start, Sufis know that God, the beloved, is purest of the pure. And they know that only a pure and truthful heart can reach this beloved. They use their love to purify their hearts. With the power of their love they shun all falseness, all impurities, and their hearts become delightful with truthfulness and light. This is often an arduous process that demands faith, courage, and total commitment to the beloved and, more or less in every case, a master. So most of them have a proper and trained guide in the shape of a *shaikh, pir,* or *murshid* (the spiritual master). Their relationship with him requires complete surrender. There were some masterless exceptions, as there always are, and they were called the fools of God.

Sufis pass through unknown, veiled, and mysterious planes and dimensions. Along the way they meet prophets, angels, saintly souls, and other highly developed beings who reveal many secrets to them and help them in their journey. This experience is always unique and gives many of them miraculous powers and a different kind of wisdom. They automatically become great healers of mind, body, and spirit. But they never use their amazing powers or wisdom for themselves. They are always used for the well-being of sick, hungry, poor, and needy people.

Most of the Sufi masters tried very hard, in fact, to conceal their miraculous powers. After reaching that most gifted state of oneness, they considered showy powers unimportant. These precious abilities are worthless for one who has become unified with his beloved.

Sufis believe that everything is a manifestation of the divine—even nothingness, even the void they call a subtle manifestation of the divine. So they accept all organic and nonorganic beings, regarding all things as beautiful and all beauty as an expression of God's beauty. Without this, one cannot approach the absolute truth.

Fakhruddin Iraqi (1213–1289), for example, was a great Sufi master who loved young men openly and was criticized by the orthodox *mullahs.* In his masterpiece *The Lama'at* ("Divine Flashes"), he wrote:

> *Although you may not know it,*
>
> *If you love anyone, it is Him you love;*
>
> *If you turn your head in any direction,*
>
> *It is toward Him you turn.*

I wish you well on your journey into deepening spiritual love. Let Ross Heaven be your guide on this journey. The exercises and wisdom you will find in *The Way of the Lover* will help you attain your heart's desire. Take inspiration from the stories of the Sufis to bring love and unity into your life. You will gain immeasurably from it.

Syed Hamraz Ahsan
LONDON, MAY 2006

Hamraz Ahsan was born into a Sufi *Syed* family and is a direct descendant of the prophet Mohammed. His grandfather was a *pir* (Sufi saint) and spiritual healer who belonged to the Sufi Qadiriyyah order, one of the oldest and most respected on the Indian subcontinent.

In his early years, Hamraz was tutored by *fakirs* (wandering holy men) and learned about the spiritual domains. In his early twenties, he became a journalist, working for respected national newspapers, exposing political corruption and gaining a reputation as a champion of freedom and civil rights. His writings drew the attention of the people he was reporting on and, to avoid assassination, Hamraz fled to London with his young family.

He now divides his time between London and Dubai, where he has healing practices, as well as teaching *Dhamal* (Sufi trance dance). He is a creative writer, poet, and columnist, working in English, Urdu, and Punjabi, and has a website at www.starmeditation.com.

your task is not to seek for love,

but to seek and find the barriers within yourself

that you have built against it.

RUMI

one

The Masters of Love

Stepping Onto the Path with Heart

> *those with mirrorlike hearts*
>
> *do not depend on fragrance and color;*
>
> *they behold Beauty in the moment.*
>
> RUMI[1]

There is a beautiful scene in the Ken Russell film *Altered States* where research scientist Eddie Jessup takes part in a sacred mushroom ceremony with Mexican shamans. Jessup has been searching for God, believing God to be only an unconscious impulse within the human brain, and he feels that these hallucinogens will help him on his quest. The dreamy influence of fly agaric touches him, and he lies down in a desert cave as a vision overtakes him.

In this vision, he and his wife share their love for each other in the simplest and most innocent of ways: smiling in a summer garden, feeding each other ice cream, and allowing openness and love to flow through—and from—them. There is a magical and transformative quality to this lyrical image: two adult children at play in the garden, allowing the breath of the universe, whose essence is love, to feed their open hearts.

The food that they share becomes holy, a sacrament, just as it would for any child bought his first ice cream by a loving father: a delicious taste of unconditional love. Freed from "original sin" and invited back into Eden, husband and wife behold beauty in the moment.

This vision takes place in dreamspace because Eddie and his wife are actually estranged, their preoccupations, fears, and the lure of academic success having caused their separation. The message is a simple one: true love is found when we get beyond the needs of the self and the illusions of the world, and find a place where we can meet again as innocents and recognize the divine in each other, in ourselves, and in the reflections of our "mirrorlike hearts."

Maybe we are all Eddie Jessup. We have been looking for love—and for God, the Beloved[i]—in all the wrong places: "out there" in the world of competition and separation instead of "in here," where the soul finds itself. Out there is fleeting and illusionary and demands that we prove ourselves over and over again to stand any chance of love; in here is a gentle acceptance of a love that is already ours.

It is not surprising, of course, that we have been seeking love in ways guaranteed not to bring it to us. This is, after all, what we have been taught to do from birth because most of us have been raised in a society where love has lost its meaning.

The very word "love" has been misappropriated by our culture, overcomplicated, and turned into a sales tool meaning something very different from "beauty in the moment." It is a biochemical reaction to a research scientist after a grant; something a cosmetic, perfume, or surgery can give you, if you are a fragrance manufacturer or a cosmetic surgeon; or a "proper response" that agony aunts[ii] and celebrities are paid to teach us about. Love, nowadays, stands for division, analysis, TV ratings, product brands, body modification—and the bottom line: how much money we have in our wallets—which is the very opposite of unconditional. Do any of us know what *real* love is or how to find it anymore?

The confusion runs even deeper. Governments tell us that for the love of our countries we must kill one another or be killed (surely the antithesis to love in any form, and an irony in itself); religious leaders preach that we must love one another as ourselves—but not, of course, if those others have a different and misguided faith and so

---

i   Where the word Beloved, rather than beloved, appears in the text, it is to signify the essence or soul of the universe that we are each a part of. If you are religious, you might substitute the word God, where "God" is regarded as an archetype or a quality of love rather than a being specific to any particular faith.

ii   A term for Dear Abby-types.

do not recognize "the one true God" as we do. How, also, do their pronouncements help us if we don't know *ourselves*, love ourselves, or understand how to give love? How, then, are we supposed to love others as we love ourselves? And what of the contradictions of a society that fosters competition and separation, rewarding its "winners" with adoration and its "losers" with guilt and shame, all the while telling us that we are equal and worthy of the same love as others?

Though commonplace in our world, these things are not love at all. True love is an energy, not a commodity; it is a force of the universe, not something to be bought, sold, or owned. Love is the ability to see with clear eyes, to allow the divine to move through us so we become the Beloved and know the deeper meaning of the universe and the passion of our souls. Only then can we be free of the myths of love and understand its truths. And only then can we hope to find it or give it to others.

Although this message is a simple one, the path to love is not without its challenges. It requires us to look closely at ourselves—at our shadows as well as our light—and to reject the myths of love that have come to control us.

For most of us, the light and the glories of love are often the most compelling. We want to be in love—thrilled, ecstatic, and cherished—but the closer we walk to this light and the more desperately we cling to it, of course, the longer our shadows grow behind us. This is why love fails so very often: because it becomes a distraction (or is treated that way) and not as a means to growth. The real aim of love, then, is not to abandon our darkness, but to embrace it, pull it closer, and love it too. Then we honor its teachings, learn from it and from our lovers, who will always—properly and by divine necessity—evoke our shadows as much as our light. Finally, through this process, we may begin to love *ourselves*.

By facing love's challenge, that is, we become light and shade in equal measure, perfectly balanced and conscious of who we are, so we can look for love with awareness and take honesty and truth into our relationships with others and with ourselves. The outcome of *this* is true love, and the challenge of the lover's path is to know ourselves wholly so we can find this love and meaning.

By doing so, we realize love's greatest lesson: that loving anyone begins with loving ourselves. And to do that, we must understand ourselves, our souls, and our needs, and realize that any love is an expression of the love that we are a part of too. True love is spiritual work, and we must become seekers on the path.

Seekers After Happiness

We come spinning out of nothingness,
Scattering stars like dust.[2]

This journey requires a reinvention of ourselves and a rebirth, too, into who we really are, not who we have been socialized into being—because until we know that, we have no point to start from and are lost and wandering, approaching love with an expectation of something else or, indeed, with no understanding of what we're looking for at all.

When I ask new students what they mean by love, for example, or what they want from it, many of them say they have never thought about it before—despite the fact that they have come to a workshop to learn how to be more loving and more effective in love. Reaching inside themselves for an honest answer, many reply that they simply don't know; that "love" is a mystery. They say they want "love" and have come to a workshop to learn how to find it, but, when asked, they have no idea of what love really means to them. Do you?

Their desire for love may be the one thing that drives their most passionate actions, ambitions, and strivings in the world, and it is the reason for our meeting. And yet, when they think about it, they have no idea of where they're driving to or what it is that is driving them.

Other students begin by repeating the myths and conditioning that their minds are now filled with: they want "soulmates" or "saviors," someone to "complete" them or to "rescue" them from an unfulfilled life. At the same time, however, they acknowledge that they would not know how to recognize this soulmate, this missing part of themselves, if they met him or her, because they have not yet explored their own souls, so don't know what is missing, where it might really be found, or what they want to be rescued from.

Some speak of wanting a home, a family, kids. But these are the conventions surrounding love, not love itself. When I ask why they don't just set up home and have kids with the person sitting next to them, then, there is, of course, always something more that is required. They are waiting for "Mr. Right," they say (a nebulous concept in itself). And how will they recognize him when they meet? Again, they have no idea, because they have not looked into their souls to understand what they're waiting for.

Every person I have ever worked with, after all the talk is done, wants to feel less empty and alone in the world, and to reconnect with something they sense within themselves but which is somehow just out of reach. In a word, they want to be happy. That is what love means on a personal and visceral level.

We were all happy once, when we were children. Even those who did not enjoy their childhoods remember days of simple pleasure because children cannot help but be part of the flow of love and to let it pump through their hearts. Happiness is in the blood of every child. It is only life that teaches us to be alone, separate, closed off, and unhappy, and to look for love and approval from others to fill the void that we feel within. This is where love's problems begin, because no one else can give us back ourselves; we have to do that on our own.

The process of overcoming our conditioning of aloneness in the world, and of finding our way to the Beloved, is love's challenge and the subject of this book. It is a process called *zikr* by Sufis, which means "remembering the truth"—that *everything* is God, the Beloved. *You* are God, too, and because you share divinity with everyone and everything, you can never be alone.

This is also a book of remembrance, then; its lessons based on the wisdom of Sufi masters who have devoted their lives to the art of love.

Sufism, the mystic tradition of Islam, emerged from the Middle East in the eighth century. It teaches that love is the essence of God and that this love flows freely throughout the universe. All phenomena are manifestations of this essence and form a single reality known as *al-Haq* ("Truth" or "God"). Sufis aim to overcome the illusions of duality and of an individual self so they can bathe in—and become—this love and know that they—and all things—are aspects of one divine unity.

The Sufi tradition originates in the teachings of Mohammed (570–632 CE), said to be the last in the line of God's prophets, who received his inspiration and illumination in direct transmission from the angel Gabriel. These teachings state that people find meaning in their lives and come to understand the loving truth of the universe by seeking their own truths.

This initially requires introspection—soul-searching and the examination of one's thoughts, beliefs, and feelings—followed by experimentation to test, through personal experience, what has been learned of the self. When this process is complete, we realize that, in fact, there *is* no self; the illusions of the world fall away, and we become one with love.

The following metaphor, by an unknown Sufi scholar, describes the method:

> There are three ways of knowing a thing.
> Take for instance a flame.
> One can be told of the flame, one can see the flame with his own eyes,
>   and finally one can reach out and be burned by it.
> We Sufis seek to be burned by God.

A number of Sufi practices have been developed to enhance this process of discovery, some of which we will look at in this book. They include:

- Meditation or *muraqaba*, an Arabic word which means "to observe one's thoughts and desires" and which consists of quiet self-reflection on the processes of our minds so we can find out what we really think. There is also active meditation, which is following one's thoughts or taking part in some activity through which God will reveal himself.

- *Zikr:* the remembrance of our true divinity, which may be achieved through ceremony, singing, devotional music (*qawwali*), ritual dance (*hadhra*), ecstasy, and trance.

- *Khalwa:* spiritual retreat away from the distractions of the world so we can focus on who we are and on our unique truths. There are examples in all sacred traditions of enlightened individuals who have found benefits in spiritual seclusion. Instances include Mohammed, who retreated to the cave where he received his inspiration; Moses, who found seclusion for forty days in a cave at Mount Sinai; Jesus, who retreated to the desert for forty days and forty nights; and Mary, whose seclusion in the Jewish temple lasted for a year.

- Plant spirit medicine and the use of special herbs and flowers with spiritual significance are also used to help the seeker develop certain qualities and find deeper meaning, as we shall see in chapter 6.

One of the greatest of Sufi sages, and the main subject of this book, is Jalaluddin Rumi, a thirteenth-century Sufi mystic and poet who wrote more about the quest for the Beloved—the great merging with the mystical soul—than anyone who has ever lived.

Rumi's poetry is sublime, his stories often hilarious and irreverent, and his wisdom simple and cutting. But I will leave the praise and anthologies to others. My interests are the practical techniques—the instructions to the Lover's soul—that can be derived from Rumi's teachings and utilized so that we become more capable of love: that special state we have all caught glimpses of, where "the Lover is consumed by the Beloved" and becomes "the soul and the universe that births souls," in the words of Rumi himself.[3]

This book is also informed by the shamanic concept of the medicine wheel. In the brief introduction to Sufism above and in the outline of its methods, you may have noticed much in common with shamanism and with other Earth-honoring or animistic traditions: the notion of a single energy (love) that infuses the universe, the idea that this can be accessed and that we can become part of it (indeed, that we already *are* a part of it and simply need to remember this), and the techniques by which we might do so: meditation, journeying inward, and the use of trance and ecstasy being just some of them.

In most shamanic societies, the medicine wheel is a tool for self-exploration and discovery that works with the four directions of east, south, west, and north, each of which has teachings associated with them. Together, these directions provide a map of love and a way back to the Beloved.

"When love and skill work together, expect a masterpiece," the English poet John Ruskin wrote. With the medicine wheel to guide us and Rumi's words to illuminate the path, we have the possibility for our own masterpiece: a life of love and happiness.

Before we embark on our journey to love, however, let us find out more about our guides.

Rumi: The Flowering Soul

Jalaluddin Rumi was born on September 30, 1207, in the city of Balkh (now in Afghanistan), eastern Persia, to surroundings of wealth and power. His well-to-do family, relatives to the king of Khorasan, were scholars, theologians, and statesmen, and it seemed clear that Rumi would follow them into a profession befitting a member of the elite.

Rumi, however, was something of a rebel, more motivated by freedom and the quest for love and truth than by social convention and the rules—and roles—that went with it—to the extent, in fact, that his behavior was sometimes shocking to his peers. When his family moved to Konya (now Turkey), for example, Rumi made friends among the merchant class—which would have raised at least an eyebrow at the time (perhaps it would even today). Imagine a child of "blue blood" and "good breeding" preferring the company of tradesmen to those of his own class. Rumi, however, made no distinction between people based on status, wealth, or fame. To him, everyone was an aspect of God and carried the same divine spark within them.

The area of Konya they settled in was called Rum, from which Jalaluddin acquired his name. He also acquired a reputation as an extraordinarily gifted spiritual teacher, even greater in power than his father, Bahauddin Veled, who was himself a revered Sufi scholar and the founder of a successful religious college, which Rumi was to inherit upon his father's death. The mystic Ibn Arabi is said to have met them both and exclaimed in joyful surprise that "the father is a great lake, but the son is a mighty ocean!"

It was in Konya that Rumi's life was to change forever, through a chance encounter with a *fakir* (a nomadic holy man) called Shams of Tabriz. In fact, "holy man" is a term that some would not have bestowed upon this itinerant eccentric. Deepak Chopra, in *A Gift of Love: The Love Poems of Rumi*, describes Shams, kindly, as "a sudden, elusive warrior who demanded everything life could give."[4] Others were less kind and regarded him as rude, antisocial, rebellious, and even possessed; at best a spiritual madman, but more likely a waster and vagabond. Still others believed that Shams, whose origins remain obscure, had been tutored in a highly unorthodox sect of Sufism that was involved with radical plant spirit practices, such as the use of hallucinogens as a means of breaking through spiritual barriers, and that this had affected his mind.

Shams would spend days in mystical reveries, lost in flight to God, weeping in the ecstasy of unconditional love. Then he would snap out of his soul intoxication and work for days as a mason, carrying blocks of stone to ground himself and restore the balance of body and mind. But he would never stay anywhere long. His name, Shams, meant "sun," but his nickname was Paranda ("bird"),[iii] because birds are always in flight.

He would arrive in a new town and a crowd would gather to hear his teachings, alerted by the reputation of this contradictory madman–spiritual genius, whereupon Shams would excuse himself for a moment and vanish into thin air, called back to the wild by the whispers of spirit. He seemed always to be searching for something: a deeper and more intensely felt connection to God-knows-what—the infinite, the void, the world-beyond-forms—that special state that Sufis know as *fana*, where the self melts into nothingness and is absorbed by the Beloved's heart.

The first time this strange and love-drunk holy fool was to notice Rumi, Shams was in his sixties and Rumi his early twenties, with a following of students himself. Shams was looking for a "master student" to whom he could pass on his wisdom, and he saw sparks of this genius in Rumi, although he ultimately judged the young man too raw in his spiritual development. Shams became intimate with the wilderness again, and the two men did not meet again for many years. As soon as they met for the second time, however, sparks flew—perhaps literally, since one of the legends surrounding this encounter is that Shams' very presence in Rumi's house caused his shelves of sacred texts to burst into flames. True wisdom cannot be contained in books.

A deep bond developed instantly between the two men, and they immediately went into seclusion for weeks to practice the mystical arts together. A deep mystery surrounds this time and no one knows, to this day, what techniques of enlightenment or magical practices were exchanged.[iv]

The social rules of the time did not support this association. A member of the elite fraternizing with a wandering beggar, even if he was acknowledged by some as the greatest spiritual teacher of his day, was something to be frowned upon, and Shams

---

iii   Paranda = "The flier" or "the winged one."

iv   Rumi was later to offer hints of what took place during his seclusion with Shams. "The one you call crazy is not really crazy," he wrote. "He's giving birth to his soul. That's why he keeps his eyes so fixed." See Will Johnson's book *Rumi: Gazing at the Beloved; The Radical Practice of Beholding the Divine* (Inner Traditions International, 2003) for a discussion of one technique that the two teachers may have explored.

even received threats that he would be killed if he did not end his friendship with Rumi.

Rumi, however—ever the rebel—would have none of this and found an unusual solution to the problem: he invited Shams to marry his stepdaughter, Keemia. Shams did so, and with that, his presence in Rumi's household was at least partly legitimized.

This was not just a marriage of convenience, however; Shams and Keemia loved each other deeply, though, sadly, it was not to last. A few months after their marriage, Keemia became ill and died, and the grieving Shams vanished once again.

What happened next is not known. Some say that Shams was murdered by those who were jealous of his friendship with Rumi, others that he became a wanderer, returning to the wilderness. Whatever the truth may be, the two were never to meet again.

In spirit, however, Shams was a constant companion to Rumi throughout the rest of his eventful life.[v] During it, Rumi established the Sufi order known as the Path of the Master, which was inspired by the teachings of Shams, and composed thousands of verses of mystical poetry. Many of these in the *Masnavi*, Rumi's epic work, forty-three years in the writing and so revered among Muslims that it is known as "The Koran in Persian," are devoted to or reflect upon Shams and his spiritual teachings. One of his other works is called *Divani-I Shams-I Tabriz* ("The Works of Shams of Tabriz"). Here, the author gives himself the name of his friend and teacher, suggesting that he is a conduit for Shams' spirit or, indeed, that he has become the master himself.

There are many today who agree that Rumi is the master of love.[vi] His poetry has been translated into every major language, and these books sell in their millions to devoted followers who regard him not just as heir to Shams' spiritual philosophy, but to that of the Prophet himself.

The teachings embodied in Rumi's work concern the notion of *tahweed* (unity), where the Lover (of life, of love in its truest expression, of good, of God, and of the self) becomes one with the Beloved (the God-energy that all Lovers aspire to).

The concept underlying this is that we all carry the divine within us, and if we remember this and find it in ourselves, there is no need to look for other gods to wor-

---

v   Jalaluddin Rumi died in Konya (Turkey) in 1273.

vi   Simply Googling the name Rumi brings up almost 4 million web pages, and an Amazon book search for Rumi highlights nearly 7,000 texts.

ship because we *become* God, capable of boundless love and connection—a "gathering of Lovers, where there is no high or low, smart or ignorant, no proper schooling required."[5]

According to Rumi, to love well may be our most important task as spiritual beings, because only in this state of grace can we forget our obsessions, addictions, and hang-ups and reconnect with our true love-energy.

And yet, loving well is also one of the hardest things we can do, because there is no formal instruction in the art of love. It is not there on any school curriculum, and our parents, having never been taught to love themselves, cannot show us how to do it, be it, or live it either. Each generation must find love for itself, which is why we so often get it wrong, caught up in dramas, misunderstandings, or even conflict—the very opposite of what love demands of us and what we set out to do—because the path is different for us all and there are no worldly guides to turn to.

When we get it right, though, love is one of our greatest teachers, giving us the power to accomplish miracles in our lives and to create our own masterpiece of living.

The Lover's Wheel: Medicine Teachings

The Sufi way—a leap of faith into the open arms of love—is an injunction to love fearlessly, impeccably, and passionately; to love, no matter what and no matter how hard it may be, even when we are bruised by the stones of the loveless, who are ignorant of their own divine spark.

Love's journey is one from separation to reunification with the Beloved: with God, with ourselves, with understanding. This union, which some call "enlightenment," is often an instant one of lightning-strike clarity and the realization of our divinity. The paradox is that this instant may take years of preparation so we are ready to receive it when it comes. Then, even a single word, a wildflower, or the flight of a bird might bring us the knowledge of love. All of these things we may have ignored or overlooked before, but when we are ready, they rush with certain truth into our waiting hearts.

Other traditions have also sensed that this journey must be taken gradually, step by step, so we till the soil from which divine flowers may grow. One of the reasons for this is that our souls have been conditioned to turn away from love, so now we do not embrace or even see it in the world. Our spiritual wisdom-keepers have therefore given us a map to illuminate our homeward journey to meet our true selves once again. It is called the medicine wheel.

The medicine wheel is an expression of the love of the universe; a mirror that reveals our unconscious beliefs about ourselves, which nonetheless guide our behavior; and a compass that shows us which direction to take so we may return to the center, the place of balance and harmony where we are of pure heart and at one with all creation: the Beloved Self.

The simplest medicine wheel is a compass with four directions, each having a specific symbolic, psychological, and mythical meaning.

The East: Stepping Onto the Path

The east is where the sun rises, and so, for us, it is the place of new beginnings, the start of our quest. It is the passion that gets things done and sets us racing into new adventures. Because everything is new, "untutored," wild, and unconditioned in this place, we can explore our true desires and motivations with purity, unencumbered by habits or expectations. Through this exploration, we learn the truth about ourselves and release old programs of self-deception and illusion that may be leading us away from love.

On any journey we take, we always begin in the east. It is the rush of nerves and joy at the start of a love affair, the excitement and anxiety we feel when we begin a new job, that sense of hopeful uncertainty when we move to a new town and wonder if we've done the right thing. And it is the starting point for every spiritual seeker.

Enthusiasm and anxiety go hand-in-hand in the east, and the trick is to stay balanced. If we allow our fears to win, then we may never get anywhere, choosing instead to turn down opportunities, refuse the gifts we are given, and stay small in the face of our loving genius. If we are too enthusiastic, on the other hand, we may rush into things without proper preparation and care, and wound ourselves in the process.

For these reasons, it is said that the challenge of the east is to face our fears; not run from or drown in them, accept them blindly, or dismiss them too lightly, but to recognize and face them. If this is done, then fear itself becomes an ally—a source of guidance and advice on our journey—and not a paralyzing force that ensures failure.

We will look more closely at fear in the next chapter, because this is our first challenge and one we must meet if we are to progress toward love. By facing our fears, we find our freedom and new possibilities.

The South: Coming into Being

If the east, symbolically, is the place of the newborn, the south is the place of the teenager and young adult: the person who is coming into being as an independent man or woman and starting to find their way in the world. It is the time when we leave home (metaphorically and practically) to find a life for ourselves and on our own terms, to start a love affair, a job, or make a family of our own.

In romantic terms, it is the deepening love, beyond the first flush, when we soften to each other and realize that there are joys, challenges, blessings, and teachings to any and all relationships; that our partners are reflections of ourselves and we of them; and that we share the journey together.

In absolute terms, the south is about the search for true and authentic power—for realizing our gifts and applying them to our lives so we can find a direction that is meaningful to us. Only by doing so can we discover what—or who—we are looking for in our quest for the Beloved.

Because of the way power is taught, presented, and exercised in the Western world, many of us never experience it authentically. Our cultural norms, rules, and laws prohibit its expression, and our institutions drain it from us. Many people enter the institution of marriage, for example, not as a result of burning love but through familiarity, expectations, or because it just seems "the next thing to do" when our college careers end and we have found the job, leased the apartment, and bought the car that we want. "What next?" we ask; "What else should we do in order to be normal? Oh yes, now we marry!"

Work is another example of how social expectations can lead us and institutions can drain us of power. Even those in happy marriages often find that, at the end of a long working day and a stressful commute back home, they have little or nothing left for their partners. This is the reality, and yet our pervading myths of a happy family and a fulfilling career lead us into these arrangements as if we have no other choices. If the objective of spiritual living (or of living at all) is to be happy, then are we really alive in this lifestyle? Or are we agreeing simply to exist?

The quest of the south and the initiatory challenge it presents to us is to realize our choices so we can understand our true and authentic power—one which comes from us and is not imposed by others. Only then do we step onto the pathway of real love and freedom.

The West: Re-evaluating Our Lives

There will come a time for most of us when we realize that what we *have* is not who we *are;* that this job, for example, though it carries great status, authority, and financial reward, is not us; it never has been; and it has nothing to do with love.

It dawns on us then that we are more than the roles we play, and we have been giving our lives to distractions and our maintenance of an illusion. We have wasted our love and humanity in sterile offices instead of the arms of lovers or the embrace of fields and forests, and now we must change the dream if we are not to waste our lives. The gift of the west is our ability to reassess our pasts and re-vision our futures so we can find the path to love, which we have wandered from.

The west represents the middle stage of any journey. It is the time in a relationship when we must either make our marriage vows or decide that this love is not for us. It is also the time of the classic midlife crisis when we wake up to the dream we have been living and can either go back to sleep or reinvent ourselves for the future.

"The breeze at dawn has secrets for you," writes Rumi. "Don't go back to sleep."[6]

There is a certain inevitability to this stage of our life recapitulations, because now we have the past to guide us and, because of this, can sense what our futures will be like. If they do not seem loving and fulfilling, then we must make a commitment to change or, as a psychiatrist friend of mine puts it, to "transform or die."[7] The death she refers to is that of the true self if we choose to continue on our half-asleep paths and give up on the possibility for a life and a love less ordinary. The work of the west, then, is to clarify our vision so we can see, sense, and seize our destinies.

The North: Coming into Truth

This is the place of spiritual reconnection, where we have the opportunity to find ourselves and embrace a life of intimacy and integrity. It is the work of realizing ourselves as creatures who embody both spirit and matter, so our souls have the freedom to shine.

Symbolically speaking, the north is the place of old age, when physicality ceases to matter to the extent it did in our youths and we relax into a new, more serene, and more soulful way of being.

In many shamanic cultures, the old are given a special place within the community because of their spiritual power and because they have made life's journey themselves, so they can advise others on how to proceed. They know something of life's mysteries, and their wisdom is invaluable. In some tribes, no one, even if strongly called, could become a shaman or medicine man until the age of forty because they simply did not have the experience necessary to be spiritual leaders and healers. The children of the tribe were also given to the care of grandparents rather than parents, because they were the ones with the real skills and the knowledge the young would need to become men and women of power.

In our Western cultures, of course, it is youth that is revered, and our elders are rarely consulted. We have sacrificed wisdom to our fascination for the physical beauty and energy of youth, which may be vibrant and dynamic but is, by definition, inexperienced and unrefined. Youth understands the world through the body, old age through the soul. For a more ensouled world, therefore, we need to embrace the qualities of old age, too, no matter how old we ourselves are; its ability to act from truth rather than expectation and its awareness of the frailty and fragility of life will assist us in understanding what really matters and the importance of love in our lives: the only truth that really matters. We will look at these things, too, in later chapters.

By working with these four medicine wheel directions and the challenges they present, we prepare ourselves for love—until eventually we find ourselves (in both senses of the term) at the center, the place of harmony and balance, where love can flower and flow.

Merging Forms: A Sufi Medicine Wheel

Sufi philosophy identifies similar stages to the medicine wheel for the journey of the soul on Earth—from raw and unformed to a state known as *nafsi kull,* where we blend again with the "universal soul" and "the whole body becomes a mirror, all eye and spiritual breathing."[8] It is in this final state of purity that the soul of the Lover becomes one with his true love.

The spiritual seeker of love takes a journey and is referred to as *salik,* the traveler. These travels take him through the stations of the soul *(maqamat),* "from infancy to youth, adulthood, and old age,"[9] corresponding to those of the medicine wheel. In Sufi tradition, these stations are:

Maqam an-Nafs: The First Step

The station of the ego, which is characterized as the soul's infancy and "the inevitable first step in life. The infant is entirely preoccupied with its need for physical satisfaction [because]…the faculty of reason and judgement has not yet been developed."[10] The route to God is through the experiences of the body, just as it is in the east of the wheel.

Maqam-al-Qalb: Feeling and Power

The station of the heart, where our emotions are the dominant force for our learning, and we aim to develop the qualities of "willpower, responsibility, consideration, compassion, and courtesy."[11] These are all aspects of power, which is the challenge we face in the south: how to find and use our powers of love effectively.

Maqam-ar-Ruh: Developing Wisdom

The station of pure spirit, where we are concerned, amongst other things, with the achievement of self-discipline and self-determination. As with the west of the medicine wheel, this requires vision, insight, and clear thinking, so we can act from a basis of loving wisdom.

Maqam-as-Sirr: Spiritual Affinity

The station of divine secrets, where we achieve a spiritual orientation to life, recognizing that social definitions of fame, wealth, status, love, and what is of value are illusions. Happiness, peace, and contentment are what really matter, and in striving for other things we are squandering our lives instead of making something of them. People at this stage of development, like the wise elders in the north of the medicine wheel, exist to be of service to others and have "a very exclusive and intimate relationship with the Creator."[12]

Maqam al-Qurb: Arriving at the Center

The station of "proximity" to God. This is the experience of the mystic, at the center of the wheel, who has found his balance and understands the nature of divine love. As I described it in another book, this is the place of "laughter and silence"[13]—a delicious laughter at the game of life and at our absurd desire to make great dramas of it when really it is there to be enjoyed; silence because, having understood this, there is nothing more to say. And, indeed, we find that in this mystical state, the silence may be actual and absolute, not just metaphorical. "Cases are recorded of some [Sufi mystics] who went for over twenty years without speaking," having no desire to communicate at all, says Shaykh Hakim.[14]

There is a deeper level to this mysticism, too, referred to as *maqam al-Wisal*, where the seeker flows "down and down in always widening rings of Being"[15] to experience holy union or "divine wedding with the Beloved."

This final stage cannot be achieved through effort or desire. Rather, the work that we have done prepares us to be "chosen" by a God who recognizes and shares an affinity with the divine spark we have lit and tended in ourselves, so there is no longer a distinction between Lover and Beloved. Our "calling" is simply a returning home, the reabsorption of our souls into the bliss-energy and love of the universe.

In this embrace of the spirit, the seeker achieves *khamush*—the silence at the heart of all—and comes to know, truly, what love means.

You may be asking yourself why—and even if—it is important to undertake this spiritual work and to travel through these many stages when you are simply looking for love: a meaningful romantic relationship, not for enlightenment or a knowledge of God. The answer is that it is vitally important if you want to find true love and not just a compromise.

Everything we do, including how—and who—we love is a reflection of *who we are* and *where we are* in the development of our souls. For example, if we are still at the stage of *maqam an-Nafs*—the east, the first step, the infancy of the soul—then our ego-needs will be most important to us, and we will be concerned mostly with the gratification of our physical desires. We will want only what our lovers can do for us.

This may be fine in itself, but not if we are searching for our soulmates, those people who will complete us and with whom we wish to build a life. In such circumstances we are torn between our desires and create confusion for ourselves and for others. Until we move on from this stage, these confusions will follow us and create patterns in our lives which leave us unfulfilled and distant from the bliss we are looking for and which awaits us.

To know love that is deep, true, and enriching to our souls, we must do the work on ourselves so we till the soil from which our flowers may grow.

The Map of the Journey

> The heavens revolve for our sake
> That is why we keep on turning like a wheel.[16]

Like all things in this world of forms, the stages of the medicine wheel that we travel through are merely descriptions; the map is not the territory, which itself defies description. But if we were to summarize the qualities of the wheel and the stations of the soul to produce a compass for our journey, it would look like this:

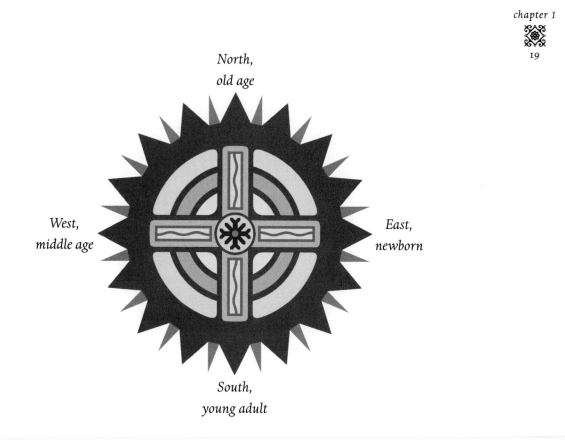
North,
old age

West,
middle age

East,
newborn

South,
young adult

The Stages of the Medicine Wheel

Direction	Stage of Spiritual Development	Attributes
East	*Maqam an-Nafs,* the "newborn" who takes his first steps on the path	Exploration of physical reality
South	*Maqam-al-Qalb,* "young adulthood"; finding our way	Exploration of emotional reality
West	*Maqam-ar-Ruh,* "middle age"; checking our course	Exploration of mental reality and the life we have so far dreamed into being
North	*Maqam-as-Sirr,* "old age"; looking backwards and guiding the future	Exploration of spiritual reality
Center	*Maqam al-Qurb* followed by *maqam al-Wisal,* "arrival"	Becoming the teacher of others

Key Question	Challenge	Outcome of Facing these Challenges
Where have I come from?	**Fear:** Overcoming social conditioning and the fear that holds us within it	The Lover is energized and set on his way
Where am I going?	**Power:** Letting go of limitations and finding authenticity	The Lover applies his energy to direct his journey onward
Who am I really?	**Confusion:** Letting go of the past to find clarity and truth for the future	The Lover attains skillful thought and so sees the truth
What have I learned?	**Fatigue:** Overcoming our sorrows, suffering, and desire to rest so we see "beauty in the moment"	The Lover achieves a shield against fatigue
How do I serve?	Holding the new dream	Lover and Beloved become one

This, then, is the journey we make in this book: from raw student to teacher, new-born to sage. The words of Rumi and other Sufi masters will guide our way, intertwining with the teachings of the medicine wheel to take us on a voyage of self-discovery into our true desires and purpose beyond all that we have been taught to believe about love, until finally we arrive at "purity." It is here that authentic decisions about life and love can be made and where we find our pure souls awaiting us.

As we make this voyage, we will explore our relationship to love, our conditioning and history, where our beliefs have come from, and—where these do not serve us—how they can be released and replaced with others that are positive and useful to us. We will then know something about one of the most powerful forces in the universe: the mystery and majesty of love.

How the Stream Crossed the Desert

ONCE UPON A TIME (which, of course, was really no time at all), there was a mountain stream: the most beautiful, clear, and sparkling jewel on the mountain where it had lived for many years.

The stream was happy with its life but had also become restless. It knew that it was admired and that the mountain bathed in its beauty, but for all of that, it also knew it was not fulfilling its talents or purpose. It wanted to travel, to see the world, not be trapped on a mountain forever. And so one day the stream ran away and, finding itself at the base of the mountain, stepped onto the plain that stretched before it.

This plain, though, was hot desert sand, and every time the stream ran onto it, its waters were sucked into the arid ground and lost. Things went on like this for many years—the stream trying to cross and the hot sands defying it each time.

In frustration, one day the stream cried out to its friend the wind: "Wind! Help me! I cannot cross the desert to see this world. What should I do?"

"Let go of your attachment to the mountain, and I will help you," said the wind. But the stream did not understand—how could it let go when it was trying all it knew to let go? And so it continued its fruitless attempts to cross the sands.

Some years later, the stream cried out again, this time to its friend the sun: "Sun! Help me! I cannot cross the desert to see this world. What should I do?"

"Let go of your attachment to the mountain, and I will help you," said the sun.

This time the stream listened more carefully and realized that it had, indeed, been holding on to the mountain for the reward of being its most precious jewel, with all the attention and adoration that brought. It was this very "reward" that held the stream captive.

As soon as the stream realized these things, it relaxed its hold on the mountain—and in that instant, the sun reached down its warm fingers and plucked the stream, in tiny droplets, up into the sky. And then the wind, whose advice the stream had ignored all those years, gathered the droplets together and blew them into clouds.

As the wind continued to blow, the clouds became bigger and began to cross the desert far below. Eventually they reached high land—another mountain far away—where they relaxed their attachment to the sky and began to rain, delivering the stream back down to earth.

And now there is another mountain stream, the most beautiful, clear, and sparkling jewel on another mountainside, where it has lived these many years, far from where it began a long, long time ago.

. . .

This story, told to me originally by Ram Chatlani,[17] a meditation master and shamanic teacher, illustrates a number of features about the way that Sufis and shamans approach the transmission of spiritual knowledge.

Keepers and Trainers

Firstly, they are both oral traditions, more or less. There is no shamanic "bible," and, while the words of Rumi crystallize the essence of Sufi teachings in all their poetic beauty, they offer *reflections* on our human condition and *possibilities* for change, not demands that we must or ways in which we should. Instead, teaching stories are used, like the one above, to suggest an approach, but the interpretation of these stories and how they might apply to the life of an individual are left to the individual himself.

There will be other teaching stories in this book, which I will leave you to reflect on for yourself. To illustrate the point, however, that these stories are in themselves *wazifa* (training exercises) worthy of reflection, the one above has as its theme the need to let go of our attachments, indoctrination, and beliefs about ourselves and our worldly status in order to discover who we truly are, the powers that we really have, and what we might become if we allow it.

The stream is "attached" to the earth because of its belief in itself as the most beautiful jewel on (and possessed by) the mountain. Perhaps some part of it even wants to continue in this way, despite its stated objectives; to revel in its glory and the status that comes from this. Mixing metaphors, the stream is a big fish in a small pond, and to surrender this means an annihilation of the self, so it becomes, in a sense, nothing. Its fears and self-perceptions therefore work against it, so at first it is unable to comprehend that it is so much more than it believes itself to be. It is only when the stream lets go of all this and faces its fears that it finds its power and can free itself to explore. *Fana*—"annihilation," letting go of the past—is therefore necessary. Paradoxically, giving up everything brings the greatest rewards.

This healing action of moving beyond the labels applied to us so we can let go of the past is a required first step in all spiritual traditions because it is the only way to be free and truly in love. Rumi, of course, did exactly this, defying social convention to befriend the itinerant Shams, a teacher whom some regarded as mad.

A similar approach is still practiced in Sufism.[vii] Syed Hamraz Ahsan, who wrote the introduction to this book, tells that every place, every street, and every town has its own "keeper" who is the guardian of spiritual knowledge. Most people would also regard these keepers as the dregs of society. They are tramps, winos, the dishevelled and mentally unravelled—and, precisely because of this, they stand outside of society's labels and attachments, and in proximity to God; indeed, it is their very "otherness" that makes them so. When moving to a new town, Hamraz's first action is always to find the keeper and to purchase his support and protection so that his own spiritual work is empowered. When he moved to London, he found the keeper in the form of a homeless man sitting in a doorway at a tube station and, for eight years, made a daily pilgrimage to this man to pay him a few coins for his continued spiritual support.

---

vii The word "Sufism" is, in fact, a new one that was coined in Germany in 1821. According to the scholar Idries Shah in his book *The Way of the Sufi,* "No Sufi ignorant of Western languages would be likely to recognize it." Other words and terms have also been applied to Sufis, including "People of the Truth," "The Masters," and "The Near Ones." Shah continues: "Sufi has been linked by some with the Greek word for divine wisdom *(Sophia)* and also with the Hebrew cabbalistic term *Ain Saf* ('the absolute infinite')." The word "Sufism" is used sparingly in this book for these reasons, and where it appears it is for convenience only.

This may seem strange to Western minds, until we reflect that every spiritual tradition is filled with such stories. Jesus was a wanderer, Buddha too—both of them "homeless" men—and shamanic tales are full of curious encounters with outsiders who have sage gifts to impart. Indeed, it may be, as Colin Wilson remarks in his book of the same name, that no progress is possible at all (spiritual, social, or cultural) without the free thinking, pioneer spirit, and fearless challenge to the norm that "the outsider" embodies and inspires.[18]

Rumi writes that:

> Everyone has a stable and a trainer appointed to him or her.
> If you break away, the trainer comes and gets you.
> You think you're making choices,
> But the trainer is actually leading you around…
> You have a keeper.[19]

Here, he uses the word keeper in two senses: one stands for those who control us in society, such as our governments, religions, and judges. They train us through their use of rewards and punishments and their application of (positive or negative) labels. Through these labels and the illusion of choice they offer us, they are "leading us around" and will "come and get us" if we try to break away and step outside of their limited definitions.

Rumi's other use of the word is in the sense of a *true* keeper, one who is a mentor and a guide to the truths and spiritual wisdom that we all have deep within us. One of these keepers is a jailer, the other sets us free.

Keepers of the truth are people we can look to for guidance in our desire to let go of attachments, because they have already done so and are free of the opinions and judgements of others, and the limitations they apply to the rest of us in how to think, feel, and act.

And this is another reason why these teaching stories are mostly passed on orally: because once written down as "law" or established truth, they become trainings—the way things "must be," which limits our freedoms—instead of *teachings*, the way things actually are.

Facing Fears

Secondly, the story of the stream illustrates two points about enlightenment that I made earlier in this book: that when it comes it may be instantaneous, but to get there might take years, as it did for the stream itself, and that there is a sort of system by which you get there at all.

This system begins with approaching our fears head-on (in this case, the fear of losing status as the "brightest jewel") and of standing alone in the world on our own terms. Only by doing so do we find genuine power, when we are courageous enough to be who we are without hiding behind a role, to take responsibility for ourselves, and to be measured for what we do, not for the labels people have given us and which can often excuse our actions.

The same message is there in the medicine wheel: that fear is the first enemy to freedom and—paradoxically—the first ally, because if we can let go of the old limitations and barriers to love, we step onto a new path, with the potential to make the circuit of the wheel and find our Beloved selves waiting at the center.

The shaman Chea Hetaka, in Kay Whitaker's book *The Reluctant Shaman,* remarks that "humans fear everything. They have spent eons learning how to be afraid. Now they must learn how not to be afraid … because they will not gain their balance as long as they are gestating fear."[20]

Fear of surrendering our pasts is actually fear of embracing our futures, our powers; of dancing outside our comfort zones and changing our present realities.

If we measure our potential for future love by our failed past relationships, for example, then we must accept our failure as inevitable. We are powerless because we have already failed.

But if we re-evaluate our past as a training ground, accept what is useful and disregard what is not, then we are powerful beyond measure. We have the capacity for love—because we *have* loved and know both what love means and what it is not. And we are also wiser as a consequence and better able to give and receive love in more depth and with greater meaning through what we have learned—if we give ourselves, and each other, permission to do so.

"A little fish was told that without water it could not live, and it became very afraid. It swam to its mother and, trembling, told her about the need for water. The mother said, 'Water, my darling, is what we're swimming in.'"[21]

It is exactly like this with fear.

The Questions We Ask Give Us the Answers We Need

Thirdly, in Sufism, as in shamanism, there is teaching but not preaching. Hence it is up to the student (the stream, in this case) to ask the questions (How do I cross the desert?) rather than the teachers (the wind and the sun) to tell their student what to do or to interfere in the process.

Even then, the answers received may be paradoxical, cryptic, or teasing ("let go of your attachments")—the point again being to encourage the student to think for himself. "Asking good questions," said Mohammed, "is one half of learning."

There are at least two good reasons for this.

The first is that we have all been taught *not* to think. Our Western education systems are based on the rote recitation of received wisdom and the ingestion of supposed facts rather than on self-discovery and reasoning.

Beneath the formal instruction, there is also a hidden curriculum in schools that teaches us to respect our "elders and betters" (to stand up, for example, when a teacher comes into class), acknowledge our "superiors" (salute the flag and the president), follow the rules (arrive on time when the bell rings and wear the "right" uniforms to school), stop daydreaming (using our own creative minds, that is), and pay attention (listen to instructions)—and there are many other examples. The more we remain in education/indoctrination, the more we are trained in this way. I know many PhD students who, upon graduation, got the shock of their lives when they realized that all their learning had not prepared them for the "real world," where they had to make decisions for themselves.

Shamanic and Sufi teaching is of a different order. It requires us to think for ourselves, so we are using new parts of our brains and developing a different sort of intelligence that is holistic, creative, expansive, and inclusive of personal choices and responsibility for our actions.

The second of these two good reasons is that the imposition of a formal system of learning onto an individual student just does not work. Rules of any kind simply cannot take into account each and every circumstance and be right in every case. We see this in the contradictions we live by in society, where our "cast-iron rules" are broken every day, often with state approval. We might all agree that murder is wrong, for example—except, that is, when the president orders it and sends us to war, or when society itself commits murder under the rule of law that permits state executions. In the latter case, we are asked to agree that murder is wrong, but that murdering those who do it is not, which makes no moral sense. There are inherent problems in all "unbreakable rules" and "ethical" systems, therefore, not least that we break them ourselves to punish those who have broken them without our approval.

In Sufi and shamanic practice, there is a system to learning, a structure of sorts, but there are few formal rules and (in this book, at least) whatever rules there are, you are free to break or ignore. This journey, after all, is of *your* spirit and toward *your* love, and we must both assume that you know your soul better than I or anyone else.

It is important for you to realize, as well, that every word of this book is merely my opinion and, since you are not me, I hope you will take what is useful and disregard the rest, for I have no great truth to impart that you do not already know somewhere in your soul. All you really need do is remember.

In Rumi's words:

> Don't be satisfied with stories, how things have gone with others.
> Unfold your own myth, without complicated explanation…
> Start walking toward Shams. Your legs will get heavy and tired.
> Then comes a moment of feeling the wings you've grown, lifting.[22]

Taking the First Step

Our first step toward love, then, is to consider where we came from, what and who we are, and to understand how our fears and conditioning will keep us trapped like streams on a mountain if we allow them to—*and to know that we can let go of these limitations if we wish,* so we make allies on the path to love and freedom.

Go well, and may your journey be filled with love.

The Birth of the Lover

Why Our Souls Fear Love and Love Fear

All day I think about it, then at night I say it:

where did I come from, and what

am I supposed to be doing? I have no idea.

My soul is from elsewhere, I'm sure of that,

and I intend to end up there.

RUMI[1]

*I*n the east of the medicine wheel, we are concerned with our beginnings: where we have come from, what knowledge, desires, and soul-ambitions we may have brought with us when we were born to this world, and the influences that have acted upon us during our early years that have taught us to love and to see the world in a particular way.

Some of these influences may be out of resonance with what we sense as our spiritual purpose—what we are "supposed to be doing"—and, through them, the purity of our love and our innate connection to the bliss-energy of the universe may become tarnished or skewed. Fear is born from this conflict between our natural selves—the spiritual beings that we are—and the pressure from others to conform to their social rules or desires: fear of abandonment, of rejection, of not being loved if we are true to our purpose and do not do as others wish of us.

The challenge of all Lovers is to face this fear. If we do not, we will find ourselves entering relationships from a basis of inauthenticity. We will not be natural or able to be fully ourselves because part of us will always be conditioned by the wishes of others. Perhaps we will be so anxious to please that we lose ourselves completely and allow our lovers to control us; perhaps, because of problems in our pasts, we will be so determined to stand up for our rights and individuality now (often without really knowing who we are as individuals) that conflict becomes inevitable in every relationship we have. In either case, we are unbalanced, and the love that we find cannot therefore be real.

The work of the east—the *maqam an-Nafs,* or station of the ego—is for us to take our first steps on the path to power and authenticity, to ask ourselves where we have come from and what we really want, and to overcome the social conditioning that has brought us here and led us away from truth. By doing so, we find new energy and our purpose in life becomes clearer.

The Journey of the Soul

Let's begin with science, since science is the mythology by which we define the world today.[viii] Our scientists offer no proof for the soul; indeed, they deny its existence, and there is no point in us making a journey to explore our souls if our souls do not exist.

---

viii A mythology is a pervading belief system that may have little basis in "fact." In constructing their social realities, all cultures take the facts that they have and "fill in the blanks" to create something that is neither entirely factual nor completely made up, but mythological in origin. Some scientists talk of the birth of the universe in terms of the big bang, for example, which they say created matter in instants. Others dispute this. In itself, this tells us that we are not dealing with a known fact, because facts, pure and simple, cannot be argued. And, of course, both groups could also be wrong, since neither was there to witness such an event—if, indeed, it took place. Any scientific theory of creation is, therefore, a myth at heart, which is only as valid, for example, as a theologian's view that God created the world in six days. Neither offers categorical proof. Nonetheless, scientific explanations have become the pervading myths (and science the new God) of our times, whereas orthodox religion is on the decline. Two hundred years ago the reverse was true—and who knows what the future holds in terms of our beliefs?

In fact, science and spirituality are a lot closer than people imagine. The contradiction at the heart of science, in fact, is that its fundamental beliefs—the basis for all its work—arise from a spiritual beginning. Underpinning all of it is Cartesian dualism: the belief that body and mind are separate and that human beings, like all natural phenomena, are merely physical entities. In this philosophy, the soul cannot be measured and so it simply does not exist.

There is, furthermore, no need for it, since dissection will reveal, for example, that the heart pumps blood around the body, the lungs pump air, and these are the things that animate us, not an invisible "spirit."

The irony behind this is that Cartesian dualism stems from the work of the sixteenth-century philosopher René Descartes, who developed his scientific system as the result of a *spiritual* revelation.

When he was a young soldier in the Hapsburg army, Descartes had a vision in which an angel appeared to him and revealed that "Nature can be conquered by measurement." Thus began his quest to prove the angel right, the outcome of which is that man and nature became things to be measured, dissected, and probed, which is where mainstream science still largely stands. All of our carving and cutting of lab rats or the cadavers on a medical student's slab have never produced a soul, and yet this approach would not have developed at all without the intervention of a soul: an *immaterial* being that could not be dissected or measured at all.[2]

Thus, science arises from spirit—and, indeed, as it has progressed in the last five hundred years, scientists have increasingly returned to the notion of spirit and now see the world and everything in it as subject to an animating force that goes beyond the physical and has an intelligence of its own. This is the basis for quantum physics and the hyperspace, string, and holographic theories now popular in more mainstream culture.

We simple folk might as well call this animating force a soul instead of a "holograph" or "string," since the word is as good as any; or, following the lead of our scientists, we could use the most common word they have for it: *energy*.

We are energetic beings, our scientists tell us, before we are anything else. The hyperspace theorist Michio Kaku says, in fact, that the human body, if all of our atoms were squeezed together, would be about the size of our thumbs; the rest of us is energy, not matter at all.[3]

This energy, furthermore, has an effect on us in its own right. Take, for example, the "phantom limb" phenomenon, where a person loses an arm or leg in an accident, but still experiences sensations, such as heat or cold, where the missing limb should be. These sensations are coming from somewhere—even though there is no "where" for them to come from. Kirlian photography has given us an idea of why these sensations arise.

Kirlian photography was invented by the Russian scientists Semyon and Valentina Kirlian. The principle behind it is that all living beings emit radiation in the form of light, electromagnetic frequencies, and heat, in relation to their internal states. The Kirlians captured and recorded these by introducing a current to the subject being photographed, which made its energy visible and able to be recorded on film.

Once the technique was in place, various experiments were conducted in laboratories worldwide that demonstrated how every living thing is comprised, first and foremost, of an energetic force that the Kirlians called a "bioplasmic body." When part of an arm is lost, for example, and the whole arm is photographed, a ghostly image appears of the missing section, exactly where it would be if it was still attached.[4]

Our conclusion must be that there is an energy within us that preshadows our physical existence and on which all things depend. For want of a better word, this energy may be called the soul.

It will be interesting to see where science goes looking for its next mythology in the decades to come, because there is a definite return, through experiments like this, to earlier practices where science and spirituality existed harmoniously together, instead of as mutually exclusive ideologies.

To give it one of its names, this marriage of science and spirit used to be known as alchemy—something which Sufis and shamans are certainly not opposed to.

Rumi's stepdaughter, in fact, was called Keemia; translated, Keemia means "alchemy."

Where Did I Come From?

Rumi poses a question at the beginning of this chapter that many of us will now ask: if this energy or soul exists, where did it come from? Finding an answer might also give us the solution to one of the fundamental problems of humankind: What is our purpose in being here?

Rumi provides what first seems a disappointing answer: "I have no idea"! But, in fact, his statement is honest, because nobody—scientist or shaman—can answer this question for us. Looked at in another way, his conclusion is also liberating because by accepting that reality is fluid, dynamic, and unknowable, instead of pretending that we are living a known and immutable truth, we free ourselves to explore and discover instead of limiting ourselves to a life within frameworks. One could say, in fact, that our purpose in being here at all is to answer the very question of our purpose in being here. We are on a journey to that answer—not, as we have been conditioned to believe, living the answer itself. Life is the Great Mystery; no one knows why or how or what it is for.

Shamans talk of "the otherworld," the spirit-place from which our souls begin their journey. Mazatec shaman Maria Sabina describes it as a beautiful and poetic paradox when she says that this world is "far away, nearby, and invisible."[5] Scientists who are trying to arrive at their own "theory of everything" use different words to say the same thing. They believe that our energy-universe has ten dimensions to it, so that reality can exist and function—the three we know plus time and six other invisible planes (which they have never seen and have no proof of, only a belief in). "Ten-dimensional hyperspace" is the term scientists use for the otherworld from which all things originate. But what is something no one has seen, has no proof for but only faith in, and which accounts for everything, including the creation of life and its continuing existence, beyond the physical, as energy? We might also call it spirit, or God, or the realm of the soul.

This scientific "otherworld" has intelligence to it, just as the shaman's does, which scientists don't understand and cannot measure, and which is greater than theirs to comprehend. Some of these scientists, at least, are in such awe of its magnificence that they may as well call it God—and some do. Dr. Fred Alan Wolf, for example, writes of this "dreaming universe" that "no forces had created this blindly, nor had mechanics created it, nor had blind nature created it. A clearly organized, intelligent, feeling, sensing, like-myself, anthropomorphic being had created it. In that sense I felt the presence of God."[6]

In the absence of any "proofs" about what this "Godlike intelligent something" might be or where our souls have come from, it is perhaps better to look to myth rather than dogma, since scientific theories and pulpit rhetoric both come and go, but in myth there is always a grain of truth that endures.

Myth-conceptions

In every creation myth of the world, there is always a time before the birth of the human race represented by an undifferentiated oneness where "God" is all there is. There are no human beings, only God-beings—if a unified consciousness can have "beings" at all.

And then something happens. God becomes lonely or curious about the powers and potentials of a God. In order to know who he (or sometimes she) is, God must separate this unified self into many different forms so he can look at himself and know what it is to be God. In that big bang of consciousness, all the kingdoms of the world are formed, and life as we know it begins.

And so it is that with God's evolution[ix] comes separation and the arrival of forms. The universal consciousness we were all once a part of is split into fragments, and our oneness is divided. This is where we find ourselves today.

Since our first realizations of this great division, humankind has been searching for reconnection with the dreaming universe, the world beyond forms, and for a meaning to life. We long to return to a state of divine and ecstatic reunion.

The prayer of Dionysius, the bishop of Athens, poignantly expresses this longing that we all might know God again: "Let this be my prayer," he writes, that "by unceasing and absolute renunciation of oneself and all things, one shalt in purity cast all things aside and so be led upwards to the Super-essential Ray."[7]

From creation myths such as these, we understand that all of life is a thought in the mind of a God we are separated from, and from mystics such as Dionysius that the

---

ix   Another of the myths we live by is that God is perfect (and therefore static), but, in fact, even in Christian mythology, we have only to compare the Old and New Testaments to see that God is evolving too—from fire and brimstone to peace and love. Or perhaps it is that we are evolving in our understanding of God's behavior and becoming more loving ourselves?

route back to this "Super-essential Ray"—the energy of the divine—is by renunciation of the self and the world of "things" (forms) in order to find "purity" and unity again. In other words, by recognizing ourselves as aspects of God, we reconnect with—and become—God once more. Rumi puts it like this:

> If someone wants to know what "spirit" is
> Or what "God's fragrance" means,
> Lean your head toward him or her,
> Keep your face there close.[8]

A reminder that *we* are God. We have only to remember.

It is still our prayer and our quest—whether we are scientists or followers of any of the religions on Earth—to reconnect with the divine by accepting where we came from and by embracing our divinity. I love the words of Irish spiritualist Michael Begg in this respect:

> We come to God in bits, dismembered.
> We don't know if the bits can be made to fit in the way they used to.
> We ask God to re-member us.[9]

The real work is to re-member ourselves, so we recall—and then live by—who we truly are and the divine we represent; to put ourselves back together, overcome the illusion of separation, and know that we are one, and that one is God.

We have accounts of what this re-membering might be like—from people who have met with God and returned to tell us of it. These people are near-death survivors.

Meetings with God

Pediatrician Melvin Morse became interested in near-death experiences in 1982, when he was called to assist a young girl who had drowned and had no heartbeat for nineteen minutes. Miraculously, he was able to revive her, and she recovered. Strangely, however, although "dead" at the time, she remembered the precise details of her resuscitation and said that while she was "away," she was led through a tunnel to a place she called Heaven.

Fascinated by this account, Morse began a study of near-death experiences at Seattle Children's Hospital, comparing the experiences of 26 children who had been resuscitated after death with those of 131 who were in intensive care but not near death themselves. His results showed that 88 percent in the near-death group had undergone similar experiences, while none of the others had.

Morse followed up with a long-term study of these children, observing their progress compared, again, with a control group who had not had near-death experiences. His results show that near-death survivors have a richer experience of living and a greater appreciation of the sacred, as well as greater compassion for others. Adult survivors of childhood near-death experiences were more likely to donate to charity, for example, to volunteer in the community, to work in the caring professions, to treat their bodies with greater respect, and were less likely to suffer from drug abuse or other social problems.[10]

The pioneer of such research, however, is Dr. Raymond Moody, who introduced the subject in his book *Life After Life,* where he recorded the experiences of 150 people who had died temporarily and been revived.[11] There are, he says, a number of things that occur in every near-death experience.

First, there is a sensation of being out-of-body, of rising up and floating above the physical self while looking down dispassionately at the "shell" of one's body. The form they now occupy is experienced as lighter and less constrained, and this is accompanied by feelings of peace and contentment.

This soul-self then takes flight, and there is a sensation of rushing through a dark tunnel toward a source of light, or sometimes of being lifted up and looking back to Earth. On the other side of this tunnel, there is a meeting with wise and loving beings, perceived as the souls of relatives or friends who are there to help.

A period of adjustment follows, and then a meeting with a spiritually powerful being who is understood to be the "keeper" of this realm and is sometimes described as God. This meeting inspires feelings of reverence and awe.

The keeper presents the dead person with a detailed review of their life so they relive it, in a sense, and see how it has been part of a greater and more intricate pattern. There may be a feeling of "karmic learning" associated with this—not a punishment or need to make amends, but an opportunity for wisdom to be received. Those who undergo this experience and live through it return with the knowledge that love is the most important thing in the world.

The emotions experienced in this other world are so beautiful that there is often a reluctance to come back, but the keeper, or "Supreme Being," tells them that they must return, that it is not their time, or, sometimes, that they have a choice to go or stay. When people do return, it is normally because they sense a need from their loved ones who are still living, and return out of duty or compassion toward them.

"Almost every near-death experiencer reports a changed understanding of what life is all about," says the International Association for Near-Death Studies. "Becoming more loving is important … deepened belief in God or a higher power is almost certain." [12]

In response to our question of where the soul comes from, then, there is no absolute answer, but from reports like these, we understand it as a form of collective energy: the essence of all living beings re-membered and returned to a Godlike state. This essence or energy has awareness, sentience, love, and compassion to it.

As Rumi writes:

> I and eternal love were born into the world from a single womb.
> Though I appear as a new lover,
> By God, I am exceedingly ancient! [13]

The lesson from these experiences (and the answer to our second question, Why am I here?) is that love and unity, not separation and division, are the most important things in life. When we understand this and live it fully, we become God's love, and this is also our gift to our fellow beings and to ourselves. Through love, and through loving, we experience our souls.

By contrast, when we remain separate from God and from love, we keep ourselves unhappy and alone. The task—and, in fact, the most passionate desire—of every man and woman on Earth is therefore to recognize our divinity and find our way back to love. This is what people mean when they say they are seeking their soulmates: they are looking for that part of themselves that knows absolute love and which they can see in the adoring eyes of another more easily than they can see it in themselves.

As Rumi writes:

> You are the King's son…
> Become a Lover. [14]

Facing Our Fears of Love

If it were easy to discover our soul-purpose, however, one imagines that everyone would do so and then apply themselves wholeheartedly to the business of living—and loving—without doubts, suffering, disappointments, or letdowns. The fact that we don't is evidence in itself that our reason for being here is to make that journey of (self-) discovery. And the first step is always to face our fears. Fear is where the journey in the east of the wheel begins.

Every spiritual tradition tells us that a confrontation with fear is the vital first step on our path to remembrance. Why should this be so important, and what does it achieve?

Shamans say that we are born with a finite amount of energy. This is our soul, part of the divine force of the universe. If we use this energy well, it is enough for us to live long and full lives, so we make progress on our journeys toward wholeness and love. If we waste this energy or use it inappropriately, however, we are less able to do so.

There are many ways of wasting energy, ranging from misguided love affairs (random sexual encounters, serial marriages, "trophy" husbands and wives, relationships of convenience, repeating old habits of attraction to the "wrong sort of person," etc.) to giving up on our spiritual quest entirely and putting our efforts into the pursuit of money, prestige, or some other worldly illusion instead. But one of the most common ways of wasting our life force is by giving away power to our fears.

Fear has become our culture's predominant way of perceiving and approaching the world. Because of our collective fears, we go to war, commit acts of "terrorism" and "heroism," "torture" and "truth," "ethnic cleansing" and "national protection," and follow dictates and dictators of all persuasions. We fear what others think or are plotting and doing against us, and we fear that they have more than us or are trying to steal what is "rightfully ours." At the same time, we fear the judgements of our leaders and the alternative as well: standing apart with no one to lead us at all.

These fears govern the ways we think, act, and feel, and mean that we use up our energy by investing it in what others expect of us. Shamans talk of soul loss, the flight from the body of the spirit itself, when we give up our power to others. Unless we retrieve our souls from the limbo they find refuge in, we do not have the energy to be loving beings (which would bring us healing in itself), and so we are doubly hurt.

Rumi writes of this that:

> The soul sometimes leaves the body, then returns.
> When somebody doesn't believe that, walk back into my house.[15]

(There is more on soul loss in chapter 6.)

Whenever we feel fear, there may also be a tendency to mask our terror with anger. In less developed souls, such outbursts can lead to physical violence without remorse for their actions; hence the drive-by shootings, gang warfare, and mob killings we read so much about. The more advanced soul may suffer shame and guilt, which will also hold them back or lead them away from love until they make amends, because a guilty soul is weighted down or seeking resolution and thereby distracted from love. Either way, our spiritual evolution and our capacity for love is diminished.

We see a typical fear response in people who have been wounded by love and make the common mistake of entering a new relationship with an unconscious (or even conscious) agenda to heal their wounds by making their new lovers the saints who can salve their pain. The outcome, sadly, is often the opposite: their pain is reinforced and further damage done to themselves, their lovers, and to others, because they have not faced their fears but looked for a rescue instead.

Take the example of a woman who was abandoned as a child by her father. When she grew up, she began a relationship with an older man. Everyone (even she) could see that she was aiming to replace the father she never knew, but no one anticipated the strength of the unconscious needs that were driving her.

The dynamic of this relationship was, of course, affected by the agenda she set and problems began almost immediately. How could she be a woman and a child at the same time, after all?

Whenever her lover played out the father role her child-self was asking for, he was labeled as "controlling" by her adult-self. Whenever he refused to play, he was seen as "unloving" by her child-self, who then went into a sulk or ran away, leaving home after every disagreement. None of them could win: the child asked for control and direction, but the adult woman rejected it. Her lover was caught in the middle. No relationship can survive like that.

The woman then became pregnant and, almost predictably, ran away with her lover's child, turning her lover, against his will, into *her* abandoning father and reinforcing the pattern in her own life. Probably she was hoping to prolong her drama, too, because, despite their separation, she continued to send her ex-lover "anonymous" notes and gifts, a part of her still wishing that Daddy would come and find her, punish her for her naughtiness, and take her home again.

This is what happens when we ignore our fears: we are not honest about—and probably do not even know—our true feelings, and so we cannot act on them and ask in a mature and loving way for the love we ourselves need. Instead, we *react* to them with violence and end up hurting ourselves and others. It is a tragic, vicious, and all-too-common cycle when our energy is given up to the maintenance of dramas, distractions, illusions, and self-important myths about who we are instead of facing our truths. No matter how hard we try, in these circumstances we make no spiritual progress, and love is an empty word.

Facing our fears is therefore the most important thing we can do as seekers after love, self-awareness, and healing.

Where All Fears Begin

> Having the idea is not living
> The reality of anything.[16]

Rumi tells the story of a bat who is informed by his peers that the sun is dangerous, so he edges himself deeper into a cave and will not emerge during daylight at all. The bat has never experienced the sun, but the mere thought of it is enough to send him scampering into the shadows.

How similar to the world we live in, says Rumi! Imagine yourself as the bat and the world outside as your playground, a land of possibility and fun, sunlight and warmth, beyond the limiting confines of the cave you are told is safe. You will never experience this playground, however, because as soon as the whisper begins that the world outside is dangerous, it becomes a fact on which everyone agrees, including you, and so you give up on your adventure without having even experienced it for yourself.

Very few of us, really, have stepped outside our boundaries to explore the richness of our reality because we already "know" that there is danger beyond our safety zones. The mere *idea* of love and sunlight, transmitted by others who have also been taught to fear, keeps us trapped like bats in a cave.

Shamans know that there is a flow of consciousness throughout the world, the thoughts and feelings of every human being blowing like an invisible wind across our planet, creating a pool of shared awareness. Jung called it the collective unconscious. Toltec shamans described it as "the mood of the world." It is the spirit of the age, the world-myth of our times, our unstated assumptions and taken-for-granted knowledge of the world, which is informed by our creation stories. We were thrown out of Eden, the gates to the garden were locked and sentries stationed there. In this view of reality, we are all original sinners, fallen from grace, and deserving of punishment by a tyrant-God. No wonder we are afraid.

As this flow of consciousness reaches us, fear becomes a myth we make real by projecting our terrors and alarms onto the world so these beliefs take shape and create what comes to be. Finally, the myth of fear becomes institutionalized, and we are taught to accept it as a self-evident truth in all of our encounters. Fear of failure underpins our education system, fear of poverty keeps us in soulless jobs, fear of loneliness means we stay in loveless marriages, fear of the "enemy" keeps our politicians in power, and fear of hellfire keeps our churches full.

Eventually, we become so habituated to fear that we no longer see an alternative. It is there as "background noise," a subtle and unconscious influence that saps our energy, makes us weak, and determines who we are. "Our behaviors and identities arise from the unique arrays of learned fears, desires, associations and expectations that are ingrained most fundamentally and broadly in our unconscious," says David Dobbs in *Scientific American Mind*.[17] And yet, for all of this, fear is not real. We *imagine* fear and learn how to be afraid.

Rumi's teachings on reality underlie the great power we have through our minds to create any life for ourselves that we wish. We do not *have* to choose fear.

This world is maintained by imagination. You call it "reality" since it can be seen and perceived, and those meanings of which the world is an offshoot you call "imagination." The true situation is the reverse. The imagination is this world itself, for that Meaning brings into existence a hundred worlds like this, and they rot and disintegrate and become naught. Then it produces a new world and better…

An architect conceives of a building in his heart. In his imagination its breadth is so much, its length so much, its floor so much, and its courtyard so much. This is not called "imagination," for the reality of that building is born and derived from this imagination.[18]

Knowing that the imagination can change our every reality, therefore, we are not powerless but infinitely powerful.

Our first mythic fear, then—and our only real fear—is the recognition of our distance from the Beloved, the divine within ourselves. This is what our social systems build upon to keep us fearful and easily controlled: that we do not have the right to know ourselves and make our own decisions, and will be abandoned by those who protect us if we do not toe the line. We are told to rely on leaders to tell us what is right and wrong, and not to discover these things for ourselves. As a consequence, our natural state has become one of anxiety, of not knowing, and a life that is fractured, complex, and frail.

Forms of Fear

This anxiety is re-enacted in the life of every growing child. At first there is only the sleeping peace of the newborn who *knows* he is cradled by life, a part of all there is. Any newborn, in his state of bliss-connection, his wonder at the world, and his still-present attachment to the infinite from which he has been born, could teach us more about love than all the words of mystics. We just need to look in his eyes, observe his unflinching passion for the world, his fearless commitment to it, and his involvement in and exploration of this new adventure he has been born to.

Sufis know this developmental stage as *maqam an-Nafs*—the station of the ego. But there is actually something ego*less* about a young child. His needs are immediate and demand attention, for sure, but once they have been met, his return to peaceful satisfaction can be instantaneous too.

There soon comes a time, however, when all young children realize they are individuals, separate from others and all other things. This is when our fears first begin—with our awareness that we are alone.

By the age of about two, there arises a phenomenon known to child psychologists as separation anxiety. This is where the child becomes anxious, withdrawn, and afraid when he is separated from the parent who provides a safe harbor from the world. By this age we have also absorbed our parents' fears of the world, their warnings, punishments, and curtailment of our enthusiasms. The world has become threatening, and its terrors resonate with something we know in our souls: we are alone in it. There is no one who really can protect us, because we are all we have. Marc Siegel, associate professor of medicine at New York University, writes that "once a person has learned to be apprehensive about something, he or she may always dread it"[19]—and so it is that we make our way in life.

How, then, do we deal with this fear in order to cure ourselves of it? How else but to forget ourselves, since we ourselves are the problem. We must, as Rumi writes:

> Be melting snow.
> Wash yourself of yourself.[20]

Our strength to overcome fear is to remember who we *really* are, that the Beloved is always a part of us, that we ourselves are God, so we can never be alone, and that this world is more than the limitations we impose on it.

> An ant trembles along with its one grain of wheat,
> Afraid it might lose that, not knowing how wide
> And covered with grain the threshing-floor is.
> Likewise, you are so devoted to your wheat-grain body.
> That's not all you are! There's much more…
> You have to experience this Truth to know what it is.[21]

The Growth of Fear

We learn fear even before we are born, from our experiences in the womb. In *The Secret Life of the Unborn Child*,[22] doctors Thomas Verny and John Kelly write that women with emotional problems during pregnancy pass on their fears to their unborn children. From the moment of birth, these children "tend to have far more physical and emotional problems" than others. The life force of the mother is transferred to the child in her womb, where she contains the fetus in the energy of her habits, fears, dramas, and emotions from the moment of its conception.

Medical science is just coming to this realization, but these facts of life are well known to the spiritual traditions. Tibetan shamans say that we are already one year old when we are born, and that "before our first breath, we have been conditioned by our psychosomatic experiences in the womb … We come into each physical life with certain qualities and habits already influencing our behavior."[23]

In one of Carlos Castaneda's books, we also read that, according to Toltec shamans, "the Level of Energy of all beings depends on three fundamental factors: the amount of energy with which they were conceived, the manner in which the energy has been utilized since birth, and the way in which it is being used at the present time."[24]

Hence, in the example I gave earlier of the woman who had been abandoned by her father and grew up to abduct her child, that baby's life challenges and anxieties have already been shaped by the mother's fears and behavior, which stem from her unresolved issues. By refusing to work on herself, she imposes the same drama on her child and curses him to carry her burdens. His life with her may be hard enough, but he now has an extra weight and a choice he must make: to absorb his mother's fears and grow up to perpetuate them, or to be drawn, without his permission, into a battle he did not ask for, in order to cast off his mother's limitations. The mother's inability to deal with her own problems becomes a form of child abuse, not love.

Family dramas like these are sadly all too common because the world does not encourage us to take on our fears or to be accountable and responsible for our feelings, and so we would rather remain in our comfort zones and play games with our demons instead of facing them with honesty and dignity.

The Mood of the World

It is not just our personal experience of hand-me-down fears from which we have to free our minds; the world has a mood to it, and this can be fearful too.

The mood of the world is the collective pool of individual ideas and thoughtforms, myths, and beliefs that create the world we know. Just as every home, street, city, and country has its own keeper (see page 24), so every person, family, area in which they live, and country they live in has its myth or mood. As we spiral out from the individual to the country, these myths become less subtle, and a nation may define itself in blunt and obvious terms (as a democracy or dictatorship, first or third world, for example); as we spiral out further, amalgamating all of these various myths, we arrive at a single dream of the world. This is its mood, which may also change over time.

A few hundred years ago, for example, the Earth was regarded as the center of all creation. Imagine the confidence and sense of well-being it must have given our ancestors to know they were God's chosen few. The triumph of science over religion has since created a new myth to live by, and we now understand that we occupy a pretty unimpressive piece of rock in an unremarkable part of the galaxy, and one we may have even destroyed by treating it with disdain. The mood of the world these days is one of uncertainty, self-protection, the dawning awareness that we are no more and no less special to God than any other species or life form, worry that the world may end, and fear of each other's actions and beliefs that might lead to this.

Our socialization into this mood begins early, when we are separated into roles and expectations, often for the most arbitrary reasons. On the day we are born, in fact, we will be dressed in colors "appropriate to our gender," placed in a crib which fashion dictates is the right one for the times, and transported to a nursery decorated according to our sex and filled with toys that are "correct" for a boy or a girl. We will also be treated differently; boys will be attended when they cry and encouraged to make their presence felt, girls will be told to be quiet and amuse themselves. From such humble beginnings we learn who we are and what permissions we have, and, skipping ahead a few years, we find boys still playing war, but this time with live bullets and dying for real, while girls sit at home quietly mourning their dead.

Nor is there encouragement for us to break free of these roles. As Dr. Arthur Janov, the originator of Primal Therapy, writes, all of our early experience, the punishments received and encouragements given, have been to ensure that we become "normal," "one of the crowd," and that we "properly" think and behave. "It all adds up to: I am not loved and have no hope of love when I am really myself."[25]

Social conventions reinforce our roles and give us our place in life. Rumi tells us of his day that "it's the custom for kings to let warriors stand on the left, the side of the heart and courage. On the right they put the chancellor, and various secretaries, because the practice of bookkeeping and writing usually belongs on the right hand."

But he also says that "in the center (stand) the Sufis, because in meditation they become mirrors. The king can look at their faces and see his original state."[26]

It is not inevitable, then, that the child in our example must always carry his mother's baggage or accept the world as a place of fear—not if he is exposed to more useful and self-aware individuals, rejects the mother's drama, and makes of himself a mirror so he remembers his original state of purity and, from there, makes up his own mind. This is the work we were born to do: to make mirrors of ourselves so we see God reflected and, through that, cut our ties to illusion and reconnect with ourselves.

The truth is that human beings do not have only one personality they must always be, one role they must play, or one drama they must live by. We are each of us legion, with many aspects to ourselves, all capable of expression, and with a potential far greater than we have been led to believe.

"The inner being of a human being is a jungle," says Rumi.

> Sometimes wolves dominate,
> Sometimes wild hogs.
> At every moment a new species rises in the chest—
> Now a demon, now an angel, now a wild animal.[27]

The trick is to discover our own truth about which of these personalities—demon or angel—we wish to be, and not let ourselves be led by others. As Rumi reminds us:

> There are also those in this amazing jungle
> Who will absorb you into their own surrender.[28]

Shaykh Hakim, in *The Book of Sufi Healing,* writes that "the first step or stage of Sufism consists in knowledge of and access to the 18,000 created worlds"[29]; to the realization, that is, that there are thousands of ways for us to see and be in the world, many of which will be richer, more wonderful, and more empowering than the one we currently dream into being each day when we allow our myths to command us and become the roles we have been given to play.

We can enter any of these worlds if we are prepared to break through our fears of doing so. "To conquer fear," as Bertrand Russell wrote, "is the beginning of wisdom."

These Fatal Wounds

> From evil eyes and malice-empoisoned breaths
> Already I have suffered fatal wounds.
> Therefore I cannot relate to thy ecstatic states,
> Save by hints of the ecstatic states of others.[30]

There is another challenge facing us when we step onto the path of self-discovery and begin to make our way towards truth and love. We take on not just our own limitations and fears, but the judgements and criticisms—the "evil eyes and malice-empoisoned breaths"—of others.

We have all been wounded by critical looks, sneers, and jibes in a society where spirituality is laughed at and those who feel its presence judged as eccentric or mad, and where love, compassion, and gentleness are regarded as dirty words. The pack who blindly follows rules sometimes does not even understand what it is laughing at, but does it all the same because it is expected—or because someone has told it to. Its members make themselves willing slaves.

Underlying the response of people like this is often their own fear of being seen as "mad" themselves and of the jibes they would receive if they broke from the pack. As Eric Hoffer wrote: "You can discover what your enemy fears most by observing the means he uses to frighten you."[31]

Such fears are the reason why lovers hesitate, afraid of a commitment that might mean a life sentence instead of a blessed union, each of which really depends entirely on a way of thinking or a point of view. We get what we believe we get, that is. It is also why projects go unfinished, because to complete them would mean a life change, with all of the uncertainties and worries that might entail. And it is why our parents push us to succeed—to protect themselves from their own fears of failure and to live their successes through us. Our fears may be the result of "fatal wounds" that go back generations in this respect and that are not truly "ours" but habits and responses we have inherited or absorbed from others.

How do we liberate ourselves from these habits of self-limitation? In shamanic and Sufi tradition, human beings are seen as having four "bodies": the physical, emotional, mental, and spiritual (the *nafas*). In the east of the wheel, we are in the realm of the physical, and it is through the body that we learn about fear and how to overcome it so it does not disempower us from love. It is the body, not the mind, that soaks up the world, discovers its truths, and remembers who we are. Children are bundles of body-energy: constantly active, exploring, and seeking, not worrying about life or getting bogged down in thought, as adults often are. To reclaim our Lover energy and free ourselves of fear, we must return to the power and passion we knew as children. This requires action: a gesture to the world that things are about to change.

This gesture need not be a huge thing, as long as it is significant to us. It could be something very personal and seemingly ordinary, because it is the intention and commitment behind it, not always the action itself, that makes it liberating and extraordinary. One of my students, for example, took up martial arts after years of being afraid of her body, binge eating, and rapid weight gain and loss, all of which had left her physically ill. It was an act of will to get to her lessons, she said. Often she did not feel like it and was self-conscious when she took her place among the fit bodies in the gym. But her commitment was strong, and she quickly developed a new trust and confidence in her body, effortlessly and healthily losing the weight she had battled with for years and taking control of her appetites and passions. Through greater confidence she overcame fear and made herself available to love.

As this example shows, willpower and personal responsibility are the keys to facing our fears. We would often rather believe that our problems were caused by (and are therefore the responsibility of) someone or something else. Whether a lover who has hurt us, a boss who pressures us at work, a mother or father who did not treat us well, we can always find someone to blame.

The truth, though, is that few of our problems are really caused by others—and certainly never solely by them—because we are the ones who accept and define them as problems. In any situation, there is always the possibility of seeing the events of our lives as opportunities rather than setbacks—as chances to shine and show love, for which we can be grateful, rather than as malicious acts that are the fault of someone else. As Rumi writes:

> Human beings are not the same.
> Some make poison for their stingers
> Others make honey.
> Some deer just make dung
> While others make musk from the same grass.[32]

The way we live our lives *is* our spiritual practice. Every day gives us the opportunity to make honey and musk or dung and poison; it just depends on the point of view we adopt. The events remain the same, but we have a choice in how to respond. Choosing to see the things that happen to us as events *we are creating*—as expressions of love and as chances to practice our loving kindness—allows our hearts and our souls to evolve so we have the strength to love fearlessly instead of holding ourselves back through fear.

> Bitter water and sweet water both look clear
> It takes one who can taste to know the difference.[33]

To help you know the difference, here is a checklist of feelings, sensations, and actions you can work with in all challenging situations.

Every event is simply what it is, and it is our points of view that make it either "good" or "bad." Our responses to such events are arisings of our own minds, links to the past and to what we have been taught to accept about ourselves, and these give rise to our actions. Whenever you experience a sensation from the column in the left, examine it (Where does it come from? What root event can you trace it to?) and then replace it, if you wish to practice your love, with a feeling or response from the column on the right.

RESPONDING FROM FEAR	RESPONDING FROM LOVE
Move away from	Move closer to
Defend or deny	Accept
Remain in a safety or comfort zone	Explore, adventure, and learn
Feel jealousy or envy	Feel grateful and appreciative
React	Act
Take cover	Take responsibility
Become a Victim or Persecutor	Stay balanced and assertive
Do it alone or manipulate others	Ask for help
React with self-protection or attack	Remain open and vulnerable
Resist change	Embrace change
Feel anger, shame, or sadness	Feel joy, acceptance, or bliss
Compete	Cooperate
Worry about scarcity	Appreciate abundance
Control and dominate	Guide and assist
Believe pain to be bad	Know that pain is just a sensation and can bring us useful information
Believe that suffering is punishment, something to be avoided, or something to inflict on others	Know that suffering is data to be accepted for what it is
Make judgements (is it good or bad?)	Make observations (does it work?)
Inclined toward survival	Inclined toward the enrichment and evolution of self and others
Isolated	Connected
Blames	Understands and shows compassion
Aware of death	Aware of life
Sees threats	Sees opportunities

Knowing that we have the freedom to choose our feelings and responses, we may even seek opportunities to do the things that challenge or scare us most, because by doing so we break through our beliefs about the world and about ourselves that lead us into limitation. Then our fears cannot consume us.

Whatever scares you most—whether it is telling someone you love them, standing up to your boss, talking honestly and compassionately to your parents about a wound you carry from childhood, or completing a project you know will have life-changing effects—do it today, or at least move closer to it.

People escape their limitations through gestures of power like these. Having done so, they eventually come to regard the fearful or hurtful event with gratefulness, as a catalyst to change, growth, and positivity which comes from a deeper purpose, rather than a wound to be carried.

> Many actions which seem cruel
> Are from a deep Friendship.
> Many demolitions
> Are actually renovations.[34]

Whatever you are afraid of, embrace it! Even if it seems unrelated to your quest for love, embrace it! Doing so will liberate the energy you need to find love, to be true to love, and for your loving relationships to grow deeper, stronger, and more fulfilling. You will make musk and honey and, in so doing, move closer to bliss.

Explorations

The exercises that follow will enable you to experience and explore the key points made in this chapter:

1. We are born in the east of the medicine wheel, but before we are physical we are spiritual beings, and we share a common energy with all other life forms. Like us, these life forms are aspects of the same loving and Beloved universe. When we see things this way, we understand that there is no separation between us and nothing, actually, to be afraid of. We are parts of the whole, the place we are making our journey of remembrance and reconnection to and from. The first exercise is a simple one of perceiving this connective energy as the life force of other forms.

2. Fear holds us back on this journey because it reinforces the illusion of separation. No matter what our individual fears, phobias, or anxieties, they are all rooted in the belief that "I am not that." We break this illusion by facing our fears. The other exercises in this section offer you techniques for doing so.

3. It is action, not thoughts or theory, that is our route to freedom, because in the east of the medicine wheel, it is the body—actively doing things—that is our greatest means of self-education.

As Rumi wrote:

> There is no worse torture than knowing *intellectually*
> About Love and the Way.[35]

True knowledge, that is, comes from doing, not from thinking about doing!

Of course, be careful and desist from any exercise if you find it too much. Then come back to it when you are ready. There is no need to rush, and you are not being assessed or "graded" on the outcomes. These exercises are for you and you alone, so make of them what you will.

Walk the Beach

In the *Masnavi*,[36] Rumi writes that "lovers want each other completely naked." By "lovers" he means not just those who are romantically involved, nor even just human beings, but every form of life on Earth that has recognized the spark of its divinity and wishes to reconnect with the source itself. By "completely naked," he means spiritually naked, vulnerable, and open, so we see ourselves and others in their essential form as the fundamental energy that animates us. Through this we understand who and what we truly are and how we are one with each other.

In these verses, Rumi tells the story of a wicker basket dipped into the sea, which experienced itself as full of water and decided it could therefore live independently from the ocean. Of course, on being removed from the sea, "not a drop stayed in it, but the ocean took it back." Our myth of separation is exactly that: a myth. We do not and cannot live independently of the source, because we *are* the source, and the ocean will take us all back. Rumi remarks on this that we should, therefore, "for God's sake, stay near the sea!"

> Walk the beach.
> Your face is pale with being so separate,
> But it will get redder.
> Paleness wants Union.[37]

This is not just a metaphor. All shamans know that where two fields of energy meet (in this case, the sea and the shore), there is always power, and this flow of power is seen and sensed more strongly. By the same token, Rumi enjoins us to

> Walk out where there's no shade.
> The network of shadows is a filter that you no longer need.[38]

A place with no shade is a desert, where sand meets sky, and where, once again, the marriage of elemental forces can be experienced. Celtic shamans knew such threshold places as doorways to another world, where spirit and matter meet, overlap, and blend. They called them "the betwixt and between" places and regarded them as "the visible face of spirit."

The simplest way to perceive the meeting of these energies is to find a shoreline (or if this is not possible, a forest or a plain), and sit in quiet meditation with your attention at the point where sea meets the shore (or earth meets sky, or the first line of trees begins).

There is a technique known to shamans as *gazing,* where you allow your eyes to go slightly out of focus as you meditate on the threshold where energies meet. Maintain this for a period of around thirty minutes. What you then see is energy in its purest form. It may appear as luminosity on the sea, or the waves and shoreline may cease to exist at all and become a sheen of power instead.

Also notice how your body feels as you continue this practice. You may feel yourself become lighter and your own energy change until it is as if you merge with the object of your perceptions and your energies intertwine. Then it can seem like there is no differentiation between you, and, in fact, that the threshold or the Void is staring at you, so you become not perceiver but perceived by a conscious, aware, and intelligent energy that is the life force or spirit of the universe, here made manifest as a wave, a tree, or a shadow.

Rumi writes of the sensation like this:

> His image kept on gazing more strongly
> And obliterated me in its heart.[39]

Continue this for as long as you wish, then relax and allow your understanding to be absorbed by your body.

What Frightens You?

The poet Marilyn Ferguson writes that:

> Fear is a question.
> What are you afraid of and why?...
> Your fears are a treasure house of self-knowledge
> If you explore them.[40]

What are you afraid of? Make a list of all the things you believe you are frightened of, no matter how simple they seem (they do not have to be grand or "cosmic"). Choose one and visualize it as clearly as you can. In your mind's eye, get as close to it as possible without freaking out.

As you do so, ask yourself when this fear first arose. Perhaps you are scared of betrayal, heights, or death, but can you remember a time when you were not?

Who taught you to be afraid? Did someone project their fears onto you when, as a child, they told you that love cannot last, that heights are dangerous, or do you remember your mother crying at some TV melodrama and learning through this that death is bad and causes pain? It is almost certain that you will recall such an event, and then you will know that you are carrying someone else's fear as an energy, not your own.

In your mind's eye, move closer to the thing that scares you most, knowing that it is a symbol for somebody else's fears. For possibly the first time, look at this thing you imagine yourself to be frightened of. If it could speak, what would it tell you about itself—and yourself? Talk with it, and ask any questions you wish. You share the same divine energy as this "other thing"; it just has a different form to you. From this perspective, we might say that, in reality, it *is* you, since your energies are the same. Another question to ask might therefore be "What am I afraid of *in myself?*"

When you are ready, thank the image-being you have been working with and say your goodbyes. Know that you can return here any time you wish and practice this meditation again, and that every time you do so your fears will lose some of their power and your heart will open a little wider to love.

Breathe

> Don't let your throat tighten with fear.
> Take sips of breath all day and night.[41]

There are mantras and simple vowel sounds that connect us to the body and to the divine within us. By making these sounds, the divisions between I and That become blurred, and we understand that there is no separation at all.

As you undertake the meditation above (or in any meditation or situation of fear), the vowel sound *a* (as in *father*) may be used. As you make this sound, you will notice that it becomes a vibration that you feel moving gently down your throat until it sings in your chest, activating your heart center to calm and empower you.

When you make this sound as you interact with the things that frighten you, you meet on the level of pure energy, becoming simple beings of spirit making their same way in this world of form.

Taking Guidance on Fear from Others

When Rumi writes that "I cannot relate to thy ecstatic states, save by hints of the ecstatic states of others," he gives us another clue as to how we might deal with fear.

Many spiritual traditions propose that the way to work with a teacher is to "absorb" them so they become, in a sense, part of you. Rumi himself says that "the friend" offers you not just advice and wisdom but "a teacher within," and that by adopting the qualities you admire in them, you "wear them and become a school."[42]

The suggestion is that you find someone who does not share the same anxieties as you—either someone you know personally or someone such as a television personality or sports hero—and the next time you feel the arisings of fear, act in the way they would.

Seek out situations that would normally cause you anxiety and enter them with the full intention to experience this fear, but wear the qualities of your mentor so you borrow their psychological and spiritual strengths. Then, as you meet these same circumstances again, gradually withdraw from the cloak of your teacher until it is just you that enters that situation. Learn from each experience and reward yourself for each step toward love that you take.

> Ignore those that made you fearful and sad,
> That degrade you back toward disease.[43]

"Researchers have known for decades that fears are extinguished not because they fade but because new, less threatening associations take their place," writes David Dobbs in *Scientific American Mind*.[44] Knowledge is power. Once we *know* that fear is not a real experience, but rather a pattern of bodily sensations, imaginings, and responses that we have learned to associate with limitations and which we have absorbed from others, then it cannot have the same hold on us.

Recognizing this, one technique is to form new associations for our fears and so exchange the unpleasant sensation for ones more pleasurable.

As an example, suppose you have a fear of intimacy. Many people do. One way of working with this is to rehearse your involvement in such a situation by acting it out by yourself, taking all the steps you would need to and allowing yourself to experience the anxiety you would normally feel. But now, as you continue your rehearsal, fade in an image of a situation that makes you happy and fulfilled. Bring it up to full intensity so the new image is bright and vibrant, and add in other pleasurable elements, such as sounds and smells and sensations that make you joyful and calm. Now you have a different association for intimacy and your body has learned a new response.

Lack of control and lack of predictability are two characteristics of all fearful events. If we can't predict it, we can't plan for it or assemble our resources to cope; if we have no control, we are in its power, not our own. Rehearsal gives you the ability to control and predict things, and with that your power is restored.

How Etsaa Became the Sun

ONCE UPON A TIME (which, of course, was really no time at all), there was a fierce snake, longer than twenty trees lashed together, which terrorized a small village on the banks of a river. The bravest warriors were afraid to sleep, for every night the snake would awake from its slumber and make its silent, deadly way into camp, where it would take the sleeping children and kill the men who sought to stop it.

At daylight, the warriors would meet on the riverbank and drop rocks into the dark waters to gauge the depth of the river where the fierce snake slept. Hardly ever did the rocks find the bottom of the black abyss.

Fear swept through the village, paralyzing the spirits of the people. No longer could they protect the children because, in the depths of their souls, they knew that all was lost. Life became meaningless. No meals were cooked—what was the point of feeding the babies, fattening them up for the snake to feast on? What was the point of gathering food from the jungle or tending fires? Love itself became a risk because those that were loved could also be lost. The people slumped into resignation and despair.

Then one day a young man called Etsaa awoke from a dream in which he saw a way to power. "Our bravest warriors together could never defeat this serpent," he exclaimed. "They have all become hypnotized by their belief that love is over and we will die. But I am ready to face that challenge."

The people tried to dissuade him, but Etsaa would not be convinced to stay. And so he stood on the bank of the river and, looking back at his people, dived into the waters and sank beneath the surface. Days and nights went by, and the people mourned their loss, for Etsaa did not return.

And then one day, after many moons had passed, Etsaa stepped back onto the bank of the river, carrying the skin of the snake. At first the people feared a ghost, but then Etsaa spoke. "This snake was flesh and blood, like us," he said. And with that, he flung the skin up into the heavens, where it can still be seen today as the Milky Way.

The people welcomed their hero with feasting, but something of the universe now flowed through Etsaa's soul, and he could not settle back into his tribe. He bade his village farewell and left them once again to become the sun in the sky.

As long as the sun shines down on us and the Milky Way lights our darkness, Etsaa is there to remind us of these matters.[45]

· · ·

three

Seeking the Beloved

Where True Power Can Be Found

subtle degrees of domination and servitude

are what you know as love.

RUMI[1]

hen we refuse to be bound by fear, we achieve a new sense of love: love for ourselves and for others. In shamanic terms, we receive a boost of energy, because some of the personal power we have been using to maintain our dramas and anxieties is now available for us to use in more positive and loving ways.

The question, then, is how to use this power: what we want and where we are going in our search for love. These are the questions we must ask as we enter the south of the medicine wheel and reach the station of the heart, *maqam-al-Qalb*.

Before we try to answer these questions, however, we need to take a step backwards to understand what power really is. Once again, we will find that "power," as the word is used in the Western world, is as confused as many of the other taken-for-granted definitions that we operate by and which tend to go unquestioned in our lives. Just as we found with "fear" and "love," when we actually look at what these definitions mean, we will usually find a myth staring back at us—in this case, one that paradoxically contributes to our *lack* of power.

Powerful Myths

At the root of our quest for love is the soul's desire for oneness, which we may recall as the security and happiness we knew as children, when we were still connected to our sense of the Beloved—the bliss-energy of the universe—and knew that we were held, safe, and protected.

In the Western world, this search for security and happiness has been corrupted to a drive for status, possessions, and fame, which is what our understanding of power has come to mean. These are not really power; they are shields against life. They do not bring us genuine happiness; instead they stoke our fears of scarcity: that we will never have enough or be good enough, or that others will not love us for who we are but only for what we have or do.

The outcome is that we covet the material—whether that is a new boyfriend or a new car—and people's reactions to us (which could equally well be envy or resentment as love) are based on our possessions, not our personal qualities. We remain disconnected from love, even though we seem to have it all.

Possessions—"things"—do not contain love or power, and they lead to powerlessness as we give up our energy to their pursuit, hoping to be admired as their owners, and always from a distance, by those who do not share the same good fortune. Ultimately this ownership is futile, because we are really seeking spiritual power, not a collection of objects. There is no soul in the mass-produced world.

Real power is a driving force toward love and comes from understanding what we want (not what other people tell us we *should* want), as well as where to find it. When we know that, we can abandon our fruitless searches for inauthentic love and apply our energy more effectively, because then we understand that our desire for riches is really a longing for the richness behind them. Rumi writes:

> His (man's) gift was gold, but Thine true blessings;
> He gave me a house, but Thou heaven and earth …
> The gold was of Thy providing, he did not create it;
> The bread was of Thy providing, and furnished to him by Thee.[2]

The Illusion of Power

People have an inauthentic relationship to power because we are part of the mood of the world, which defines power in terms of the material, and it is easier to measure wealth than the depth of the soul.

The consequence of this is that we do not know what real power is because we have never been taught to recognize it. In school, work, and our other social systems, we are told that power equates with performance—doing what we are told, quietly and unobtrusively producing answers that support the majority view, and achieving measurable results on which our material rewards can be based. Through our acceptance of such definitions, we end up *dis*empowered because we are always acting for someone else and in ways that they approve of, whether they are meaningful to us or not.

Nor do we receive the support and guidance we need to find answers of our own, because the role models society offers us have given up their power too. "Making a mark on the world" is not about individuality, inspiration, and following our dreams, but sacrificing our individuality so the system can survive and consume the power of others.

For these reasons, those whom we regard as most powerful and whose lifestyles we aspire to have little power themselves, ironically. Every politician, businessman, or celebrity knows the truth of this. Their days are dictated to them, filled with performances, appointments, and protocols. Managers and civil servants control their decisions, spin doctors tell them who they are and what to say, and their nights are filled with worry over deadlines, appraisals, and promotions, so they are not even free to dream. This is what we are taught to hunger for—and, once we get there, we are told to maintain the illusion, so that those outside our circle do not see how powerless we really are.

This is the realization that Jake Horsley came to.[3] "I was born into money," he writes. "At eighteen, I inherited shares in the family business worth half a million pounds. The dividends alone came to around £20,000 a year; back in 1985, a tidy sum indeed." Jake set about doing what many of us might in a similar situation. On an average day he got up at 1 PM, drove into town, spent £200 on CDs, rented three or four movies, and spent the rest of the day smoking joints, drinking tequila, and getting high. "What no one saw, however, was that I was crying myself to sleep at night. What I wanted most of all was simply to fall in love … My life of luxury seemed a cruel mockery, since I could have everything except the one thing I wanted."

Jake's solution was radical and brave. He sold his shares and put the money into land, which he then signed over to a friend. He gave away his belongings to a relative. He kept about £1,000 for himself, but gave away half of it to people he met on the streets. Then he said goodbye to everyone and everything he knew and got on a plane to Morocco, although it could have been anywhere. "When you leap into an abyss, you don't have to take aim," he said. "I was fleeing from my life, and anywhere alien to my Western sensibilities would do. I wanted to be reborn; I just didn't want to have to die first."

The outcome was that Jake finally found himself and began to love life. "I was free to reinvent myself, with no one to tell me otherwise … This was what I had chosen to be." He is now an author, following his dream and living on his own terms.

"For the record, I never regained my wealth, nor regretted throwing it away … With hindsight, it was less a whim that made me do it than simple self-preservation. Today, I live, just barely, off the proceeds of my books, hand-to-mouth, and one day at a time." But each day is rich and real and filled with the authentic power of a life chosen and lived, not drifted through, and with the potential for love and greatness.

In contrast to Jake's experiences, where freedom was fought for and gained, many of us do drift through life, never seeking our true power, not even aware that it is possible to step outside of our social programming. We become complacent, content to absorb and live by the rules we have learned, always asking permission.

A humorous example is a student of mine who was undertaking a visionary ceremony with twenty others one night, an exercise to instill insight and illumination. The visions did, indeed, arrive for this student, but in the morning she was disappointed. "Every time I started to see a world beyond forms, the room was too bright and the visions went away," she complained. "Perhaps next time you could black out the windows and put up curtains to block out the light of the moon."

I answered that it would be possible, of course—or she could just close her eyes! "Oh," she said. "You didn't say I could do that!" When we have to ask permission to even close our eyes and allow our bodies to respond naturally to the world around us, we know for sure that we have absorbed too many rules.

Psychologists working in the field of human potential and creativity are concerned by our willingness to give away power. They worry that if we are conditioned to this extent, then the creative impulse on which progress, evolution, innovation, and love itself depends will also become stifled, leading to stagnation.

Ulrich Kraft, in his article "Unleashing Creativity,"[4] writes that "we start our young lives as creativity engines but our talent is gradually repressed.

"Schools place overwhelming emphasis on teaching children to solve problems correctly, not creatively. This skewed system dominates our first twenty years of life: tests, grades, college admissions, degrees, and job placements demand and reward targeted logical thinking, factual competence, and language and math skills—all purveys of the left brain.

"The propensity for convergent thinking becomes increasingly internalized, at the cost of creative potential. To a degree, the brain is a creature of habit; using well-established neural pathways is more economical than elaborating new or unusual ones. Additionally, failure to train creative faculties allows those neural connections to wither. Over time it becomes harder for us to overcome thought barriers."

We become led by habit, controlled by others, giving expected responses and not standing in our power or experiencing the world, creativity, and love in the fullness available to us.

It is interesting that Kraft's time frame for this indoctrination is the first twenty years of life, because during this time we are also, chronologically speaking, in the south of the medicine wheel and most concerned with issues of power. It is now that we are exploring, trying to make sense of the world, leaving school, finding lovers, saying farewell to our parents, and making homes, careers, and futures for ourselves.

Our tendency, however, will be to *renounce* power by allowing ourselves to be defined in terms of salary or status, because this is what we believe power to be. But this is not finding ourselves, it is giving up our passion and individuality for illusory rewards. If we wish to find genuine power, then we must, as Rumi says, push the hair out of our eyes,

> Blow the phlegm out of your nose, and from your brain.
> Let the Wind breeze through.
> Leave no residue in yourself from that bilious fever.
> Take the cure for impotence, that your manhood may shoot forth,
> And a hundred new beings come of your coming.[5]

One of the things that makes it difficult for us to extract ourselves from this "bilious fever" of social expectations is that we are preconditioned to give up power to others. Our first jailers in this respect (often unconsciously and with the best of intentions) are, in fact, those who love us most: our parents.

Grabbing Power from Others and Losing It for Ourselves: Family Scripts and Dramas

We are all subject to life scripts that we inherit from our parents. Like fear, these begin in the womb, as our parents project onto us the myth or drama that is taking place in their own lives. This drama is their response to the things they have been taught about life and the ways of behavior they have learned from their own parents. Thus, these scripts often go back generations to an original experience or problem that created the imbalance being carried forward.

Parental myths can have a huge impact on the lives of children. Unless the child or the parent can make them conscious and see them for what they are, these myths will continue unconsciously to drive that parent's behavior in the upbringing of their son or daughter, as well as the child's behavior in response to the myth imposed on them.

For example, your mother may have learned from her own mother that she was unwanted and unloved, perhaps through something as subtle as a turn of phrase or a denial of affection at a crucial moment when she needed comfort. Through this she may have come to believe that *all* children are unloved and a burden on their parents. This program runs in the background even if your mother consciously wanted you very much when she conceived you. It will subtly affect her behavior as she goes about her parenting, perhaps coming to the fore when she is tired or under stress and you make demands on her energy. At those unthinking moments, she may react from habit and repeat the behavior she has learned from her own mother, forgetting the effect it had on her.

Miguel Ruiz, in his book *The Four Agreements*, provides an example of how subtle this process can be. It is the example of a young girl who was singing and playing one day when her mother arrived home from work. The mother, fatigued and with a terrible headache, tired from her work and feeling irritated, eventually had enough of her child's joy and exuberance and yelled at her to "shut up! You have an ugly voice."

The girl, says Ruiz, then came to believe that her voice was "ugly and would bother anyone who heard it…even though she had a beautiful voice, she never sang again… this spell was cast upon her by the one who loved her the most: her own mother." [6]

Another example comes from one of my students, who "knew" she was unwanted because her father had left her and her family when she was young, going on to have a daughter whom he actively parented with his second wife. This left my student in the care of a woman who was, by implication, unsatisfactory in some way (or why would her father have gone?).

An undercurrent of anxiety and unanswered questions thus surrounded her life, and her search for love was impaired by this. By the age of thirty, she had allowed herself to become pregnant six times; four of them aborted in as many months because they were also unwanted. Two of them, however, were so badly wanted that she removed them from their (two different) fathers so she could control them and keep them close; then they would never leave her as she had been left.

Her life, in effect, was chaotic. Her myth and that of her family centered on what it means to be "wanted" or "unwanted," and while it continued to play out in her unconscious mind, she could not grow up into adult power or take responsibility for herself and the emotional well-being of her children. Instead, and now without fathers, they were primed to play the same drama too, because the child of an "unwanted" mother carries this "unwanted" quality in his cells. He will not have a name for this feeling, but he will feel it nonetheless in the mood that hangs over his life.

In ways such as this, subtle energies can lead to unhealthy expressions in our relationships if we do not seek our power and free ourselves from ancestral wounds.

"Because we are decent, basically good people, we ourselves can sort out what to accept and what to reject," writes Chodron. "We can discern what will make us complete, sane, grown-up people, and what—if we are too involved in it—will keep us children forever. This is the process of making friends with ourselves and with our world. It involves not just the parts we like, but the whole picture, because it all has a lot to teach us."[7]

The Shocking Conclusion

The psychologist Stanley Milgram, on the other hand, showed disturbingly where the theft of our power by others and our lack of connection to love might lead us if we do not sort out what to accept and reject.[8]

Milgram wanted to know why ordinary, decent people went along with the atrocities of World War II, when millions were killed in death camps by soldiers who were "just following orders." The answer, he believed, was that absolute obedience to authority, to the detriment of love, was something we learn as we grow up.

Between 1960 and 1963, he carried out a series of tests involving more than 1,000 people in which participants were given roles of teacher and student. The teacher's job was to administer an electric shock every time the student made a mistake in a simple learning task.

The student was strapped into an electric chair and told to memorize pairs of words, while the teacher sat in front of a shock generator with thirty levers on it, marked from 15 to 450 volts, the last of which was labeled "Danger: Severe Shock."

To begin with, the student (actually an actor employed by Milgram who did not really receive a shock at all) answered correctly, but then began to make mistakes. As the voltage level increased, he started to complain, then shout. At 300 volts, he screamed and said his heart was bothering him. At 315 volts, he made no further sounds at all. The experiment continued until the teacher refused to pull another lever or until he or she reached 450 volts and gave this shock four times, one after the other.

In similar circumstances, I suppose we would all like to think we would refuse to give any electric shocks at all. Few of Milgram's subjects did, though. All of them went to at least 300 volts, and almost two-thirds (65 percent) went to 450 volts. When someone else gave the shock for them at their command, a staggering 92 percent complied. Even when the teacher was told to physically hold the student's hand on the electric plate, 30 percent of them did.

Milgram's conclusion was that we are all prepared to act without love when someone we believe to have more power than us demands it, because we have been taught to do so all our lives.

Another view on this is provided by Patrick Obissier in his book *Biogenealogy*.[9] Obissier is a medical doctor who noticed that emotional stress was at the root of every illness he treated, and that this could be traced to the history of his patient's family. Adherence to family scripts actually led to physical illness as the unresolved issues of the parents and grandparents became part of the cellular memory inherited by their children and continued to trigger illnesses in the generations that followed. Diabetes, for example, which creates excess sugar in the bloodstream, was triggered by feelings of powerlessness. The body compensated for its lack of power by manufacturing more sugar than was needed to fuel the muscles.

To stop this excessive sugar production, the psychic distress beneath the process had first to be resolved by re-empowering the patient so the disease itself (as well as the emotional problems underlying it) would not be passed on to the next generation, who would inherit their parents' lack of power.

By discovering solutions to create harmony and give his patients emotional strength, Obissier noticed that they no longer created disease, and illness was no longer the bequest they left to others.

It *is* possible to free ourselves from such life scripts—though it will take work—by making a conscious decision to live in the *now* instead of the past. Waking up to Grace, letting go of our histories, our life *stories*, and sensing that we live each moment in the presence of a greater love, is what it takes. Rumi tells us:

> This is how a human being can change:
> There's a worm addicted to eating grape leaves.
> Suddenly, he wakes up, call it Grace, whatever,
> Something wakes him, and he's no longer a worm.
> He's the entire vineyard, and the orchard too, the fruit, the trunks,
> A growing wisdom and joy that doesn't need to devour.[10]

The following meditations will help you explore your own life scripts and call to the power of Grace, so you have a basis for change and can reclaim your energy from others.

Meditations on Not-Being

> Take someone who doesn't keep score,
> Who's not looking to be richer, or afraid of losing,
> Who has not the slightest interest even in his own personality:
> He's free.[11]

When we enter a space of meditation or quiet self-reflection, we are able to let go of the outside world and all the power games and competitive dramas it imposes on us. Our minds can regroup for a while.

Meditation is like choosing to explore the world in a different way, by going through a new mental doorway instead of the one we habitually use to perceive and make sense of our lives. Scientists tell us that one half of our brains (the dreaming, intuitive, creative side) is barely used in our daily lives; instead we engage the world through the "rational" side, which is that socialized part of ourselves that has been taught to respond in terms of right and wrong, guilt and blame, and all the other judgements that feed into our life scripts.

In meditation, by contrast, we discover something of our essential selves—who we were before we were told who to be—and we take power from this, so we recharge the batteries of our souls.

Shamans call such exercises a "not-doing." If our habits and unconscious actions— our "doings"—are reflections of our dramas and scripts, then stepping outside of these roles and expectations is a not-doing, a gesture of freedom through which we explore our potential beyond the things we are used to.

In normal meditation, the aim is to recognize the arisings of the mind, the constant flow of momentary thoughts that skip across it, and to let these go as "thinking." Shamanic meditation is more active than this, however, because the intention is to enter the meditative state with the aim of exploring these thoughts, not ignoring them.

Intention is an act of will; it is the setting of an agenda for self-exploration, so we go into meditation with the purpose of using these thoughts to shed light on our souls. When a thought train begins, therefore, we follow it and observe where it leads, watching as a symbolic journey unfolds, myths are revealed, and metaphors—the language of the unconscious mind—tell us more about who we are.

The process is fascinating because it shows that these deep thoughts, these arisings that we are told to ignore in daily life, are actually the things that really determine our behavior. They *are* us. Because we do not normally notice them, however, we have little idea of what really motivates us, of whose voice we hear in the back of our minds telling us what to do, or that our actions are often actually *reactions* and out of our control.

What you may also discover in your active meditations is that you are many people, all of whom have had (and continue to have) input to the creation of this person you believe yourself to be. There may be many voices in your head, and even arguments going on between them, as these different forces try to influence your behavior and pull you in competing directions.

If we do not even know these voices exist, then of course our actions will be confused. Without a clear focus on where we are headed, our power and connection to love can be taken from us as we get lured into the games of others (see next chapter). Through active meditation, however, we become "not-beings,"

> Mirrors of the Beauty of all things.
> Because Not-being is a clear and filtered essence
> Wherein all these things are infused.[12]

Some of the questions you might take into your meditation as your intention for this work could include:

What Makes Me Sad?

The world was not made for sadness. We are not the original sinners we believe ourselves to be, and we are not being punished by God. We can have anything we want; it is all within our power. There are plenty of stories of people who have achieved their dreams by overcoming self-limitations. "If you believe you can or believe you can't, you're right," as the businessman Henry Ford put it.

So what makes you sad? Most likely your sadness will be for something or someone you do not have, or once had and have now lost.

This separation from love is illusion. Our lives are touched by others in many ways, each of them perfect in itself, bringing what we need at that time. Living is a process of change and growth, and we are all on our way back to the source, helping each other as we go. Nothing is lost forever, and we can let go of our sadness around our perceived losses and wounds if we accept the possibility of perfection and change.

> How to cure bad water?
> Send it back to the river.
> How to cure bad habits?
> Send me back to you.[13]

Sadness is a "bad habit" we fall into, and the way to cure it, like the "bad water" Rumi writes about, is to send it back to the river; to reconnect with the source and embrace the unity that underlies all of the things we will touch and be touched by in life.

One visualization practice *(wazifa)* is to mentally make a list of the things that sadden you, wrap it in healing light, then let it go to the universe. This exercise is a gesture that then requires a follow-through action, "because Sufism is action, not institution," as Idries Shah writes. "No Sufi sets up an institution intended to endure."[14]

Once we have let go in our minds of the things that make us sad, we need to go out into the world with a commitment to make things change. It is easy to lose ourselves in descriptions—that we are "lonely," "overweight," or "unloved," for example; descriptions which become ingrained habits in the way that we see the world and the way we behave within it. Our descriptions become self-fulfilling. The warrior commitment, instead, is to dare take a chance on doing something different: join a club, a gym, or a dating agency. What do you have to lose, after all? Only your sadness.

The most positive thing you can do—for yourself and for the world—is to be happy. Simply let your sadness go, even if it requires an act of will, because *being* happy *creates* happiness, and you become the change you wish to see.

Of What Am I Ashamed?

> Water says to the dirty, "Come here."
> The dirty one says, "But I am so ashamed."
> Water says,
> "How will you be made clean without me?"[15]

Almost certainly, we have all done things in pursuit of power that, when we wake up to the truth, cause us shame—shame for all that we have lost of ourselves and given up of our humanity, for how we have been tricked by the game, and for the things we have done in our blindness. If we allow this shame to dominate us, however, we will limit our power still further, as well as our opportunities to find our way back to love.

Two responses are common when the weight of shame is felt by the soul: one is despair, the other violence.

Despair is a loss of spiritual power caused by our recognition of the harm we have done to others. It is detrimental to us in equal measure to the harm we have caused, and in order for us to recover our power before we are led into further sorrow we must make amends for our actions by compensating those we have harmed. At the very least, this means remembering them in our prayers. And then we must learn from our actions so we do not make the same mistakes again, because in the end it is our souls which suffer.

For any situation in which you feel despair because you have not acted with spiritual integrity, take one loving action of generosity and kindness, patience and compassion toward another person. You will feel your soul healing with every gesture of love, because you are clearing your own emotional blockages so the greater soul of the universe can flow through yours and reclaim you.

Another response to shame is to act with greater violence. This is truly unhelpful and will wound us (and others) still further, but it is a common reaction, the underlying belief being that since we have involved ourselves in spiritually harmful behavior, we are already "lost" and may as well "be hung for a sheep as a lamb." The truth is that we are never lost. However, aggressive behavior—which is often a mask for sorrow rather than anger—will prevent us from being found, or, that is, from finding our true selves again.

One of the physical outcomes of anger is that we can burn ourselves up. I find with my healing clients that those who have a lot of "heat" in their bodies (expressed as eczema, asthma, lupus, auto-immune problems, and so on) often have unexpressed anger at the root of their illness, and it is this anger that needs to be released in a constructive and creative way so it does not continue to manifest as a self-harming illness.

We can have a lot invested in carrying anger as illness. Sometimes we cling to it as a punishment to others (which is violent behavior in another form). If we are angry at the way we have been treated by our lovers, for example, but feel unable or unwilling to deal with the issue directly, we can burn ourselves up and become ill, as if to show them the consequences of their actions: "See how sick and unhappy you've made me." Of course, this is also self-defeating, because we are the ones who suffer—doubly so, in fact, because we do not give our lovers a chance to learn from their mistakes or make amends toward us either.

If your meditations on shame reveal anger you are carrying, then it can and should be released. You can do so in a calm and controlled way by simply stating your case to the person with whom you have the issue, or you can expel it from your body by really letting go. In the latter case, it is a healthy practice to go out into nature and find a place where you will not be disturbed, then scream and rage all you wish until you have let your anger out. What you may then find is that your sorrow has a chance to express itself and your tears can start to flow. This is the greatest healing because, with the water of tears, you put out the fire of your rage, and in so doing you reclaim your power from the person or event that engendered this feeling in you.

As one of my students remarked about this practice:

"When I kept the tears inside me, I became bloated. The waters of unexpressed sadness combined with the fire of my anger, and I was always 'letting off steam'!

When I was able to cry, I saw how my rain of tears helped my flowers to grow."

What Is the Worst Thing That Ever Happened to Me?

To awaken from the "illusion of being alive" is to experience life itself. The past is a dream. Human beings simply do not have the mental capacity to recall every event that has ever happened to them and which has combined with others to create the story of who they are. Some of these things (such as their experiences of the womb and early childhood) are consciously unknown to them anyway, and those they do recall are often remembered incorrectly. Studies show that eyewitness testimonies, even of a dramatic event like a robbery, which is unusual and sticks in the mind, are incorrect in more than half of all cases.

Since we can't recall everything from our lives, our life stories are dreams as well. If you try, you can select from your life events that tell your story as a hero, victim, abuser, or abused. Even the same event, looked at from a different perspective, can make you a saint instead of a sinner. "I can't say what has happened," writes Rumi. "What I'm saying now is not my real condition."[16]

The real question, then, is: "What have I invested in perpetuating this particular story and carrying this myth with me?" Given that you can be anyone you choose, why do you choose *this* person?

When you think about the worst thing that has ever happened to you from this perspective, you can, in a sense, see the contract that was in operation at the time between you and the event itself. There are few genuine accidents or coincidences; instead, the roles we play and the stories we live lead us to the people and events that reinforce these stories themselves.

The worst thing that happened will be something that caused your power to be lost. Given that this circumstance was not entirely accidental, what was its purpose and what was your part in it? What patterns in your life does it represent (and has such an event happened before or afterwards)? What does it tell you about yourself, your story, and the circumstances in which you give up your love and power?

Most importantly, how could things have been different and, knowing that they can be, what will you learn from this event so that things will be different in the future, and you can retain your connection to love?

What Do I Deserve?

> Our forms are only as waves or spray thereof.
> Whatever form the ocean uses as its instrument,
> Therewith it casts its spray far and wide.[17]

Our stories, our pervasive myths, cause us to draw in the things that support our roles. All events and happenings are, in this sense, the props of an actor: just waves and spray, and even when the things we attract are detrimental to us in some way, we would rather be good actors than change the script.

At a workshop in Ireland, I once said to the group that, through an act of will, any person there could have anything or be anyone they wanted. Immediately, I was met with uproar. "What do you mean, I can have anything I want?" demanded one woman. "What if I desire a lover but the man I attract is abusive?" The question said more about that woman's story and the barriers she was putting up to love than it did about any risk from men, because if she could have *anything* she wanted, why would she *choose* an abusive lover?

What we all deserve is love, happiness, and a return to the arms of the Beloved. Anything that stands in the way of that possibility is an illusion, but we have free will and can therefore choose illusion over truth and fear over love if we wish. The choice that we make may be based on our life script, but we have the ability to rewrite that too and choose a different story.

What, then, do you deserve? What are you worthy or not worthy of? Who told you these things and do you really choose to believe them?

What is to stop you having the things you want and deserve? It is self-belief alone that permits or denies you these things. Consider a different story. What part would you like to play, and how would you like this new and more positive story to unfold?

What Is My Myth of Myself?

> When you eventually see through the veils
> To how things really are,
> You will keep saying again and again,
> "This is certainly not like we thought it was!"[18]

The purpose of meditations like these is to bring us closer to the truth about ourselves and to the realization of those "18,000 worlds" within us—that we are not fixed in one story or role but have infinite potential for change.

All of our stories are driven by an underlying myth that can be explored further to see what we are acting out and where this dream of ourselves has come from. The way to do this is simply to make a statement about yourself and then to ask in your meditations, "What is beneath this statement—this belief about who I am?"

In the example of the Irish woman above, for example, we might say that her statement about herself is: "I always attract men who hurt me."

So, what is beneath this, and where does such a belief come from? The answer might be: "Because all of my relationships with men have been this way."

But what is beneath that? Does it mean that things must always be this way? Since she is aware that her relationships generally go badly because of the men she attracts, why does she continue to attract—and, more to the point, *be attracted to*—such men?

Asking questions such as these, we might eventually arrive at the conclusion (as was the case in this example) that this woman had a myth of herself as a victim; unlucky in love, always at the mercy of, and knocked back by, life.

The questions can then continue: "So what is beneath that—where does this myth come from?" The answer in this case was: "From my mother. When I was a child, I was always told not to want too much. 'I want doesn't get' was one of her favorite expressions. Whenever I was happy and laughing, she would tell me to be quiet; when I got a boyfriend, she told me it wouldn't last, or to be careful, to watch out for my heart, that men were only after one thing."

The mother, in this woman's life, had projected her own fearful myths onto her child. Anxious to prove her mother right, the daughter had created the reality her mother wished to see.

The point, though, is that the mother's myth is not the only possible truth; it is the daughter's *living of it* that makes it real. In this way, the child gives her power to the parent and suffers the consequences of her mother's fears, which may or may not even have been true for the mother, since they are mythological too. Even if they were, they were the experiences and fears of mother, not child, until she imposed them on her daughter through careless remarks, and her daughter decided to believe them.

Projections like these, of our myths onto another, are of two types:

There is a simple form of projection where we see in the world and in others the things that we know to be true about ourselves, even if this knowledge is largely unconscious. A student of mine, for example, got involved in a legal case against her ex-partner. To help her case, she told the court that her ex was a drug user. Not only was this not true of him, but he was able to show the judge a letter this student had written him offering to sell him cannabis! She was actually the drug user, but in the drama she had built around herself, perhaps she really couldn't see the facts of the matter. It is easier to accuse others of what we most fear or cannot face in ourselves than to be free of illusions and act from the remembrance of love.

Another form of projection is where we transpose onto the world the things that we know ourselves *not* to be. As an example, another person I worked with presented himself to the world as a very spiritual and upright man. All of his words were of the beauty of nature, the sacred it embodied, and how it should be trusted. Yet in his business affairs and relationships, he involved himself in deception and the misappropriation of other people's work. Sacredness and trust were the very issues he was struggling with. He would have loved to have been these things that he saw in the world, but in his deepest soul he knew that he was not, and so he pretended they were true, living his self-deception and deceiving others that he was a man of great spiritual worth. This is one step away from being a con artist, the difference being that the con man is conscious of what he is doing while the self-deceiver is not.

Beneath all of these self-deceptions, projections, myths, and the twists and turns of the dramas they get us into, there is one simple fact: *we do not know anything for certain*. Not even who we are.

And this is what offers us our greatest freedom: if nothing is fixed and known, then we are free to be anyone and to have anything we truly want if we earnestly seek our truths and commit ourselves to living them.

What, Then, Is My Not-Being?

> When you look in a mirror,
> See yourself, not the mirror.[19]

If the myth we have accepted about ourselves is our "being," then our not-being is our possibility—our "one square centimeter" for change, in Castaneda's words—of choosing something better.

One way to explore this is to write out the story of your life as if it *were* a story. How does it begin? Who are the main characters? How do they interact with you? What is the mood of the piece (comedy, tragedy, drama, farce)? What is your role? Which scenes have been played out already? How do you see the drama unfolding from now on? What is the ending like? All of this is information from your soul about the life you are living and the story you are a part of.

If you're happy with the drama and its outcome, then you may not need to change anything. Know that it's a game, but if you're not hurting anyone else or yourself, carry on playing. Because we are alive, we have to do something, after all. Of course, agreeing to play only one part when you could be anyone does limit your possibilities, but if your life works for you, perhaps there is nothing to fix.

On the other hand, since you're reading this book, you are probably looking for answers because something isn't working—in which case, try varying the story. Write it again, and this time take a different role or give it another outcome. If you'd prefer the story of a saint to that of a sinner, write it that way and then play that part instead. Your story is your mirror, but it is only by living it differently that you see yourself and not the mirror in which you are reflected.

Questions like these (and they are not the only ones you might ask in your meditations) reveal how we see the world, and through whose eyes, really, we see it. While we remain unknowing, we are the agents of other people's thoughts and the beliefs they have instilled in us. We then project these onto the world and turn it into our reflections. The point, then, is to become "selfless" by refusing to allow these scripts to play out in our heads. When we choose selflessness, we allow the divine to flow through us, and we become clearer channels for the love of the universe.

A Selfless One disappears into existence and is safe there.

He becomes a mirror.

If you spit at it, you spit at your own face.

If you see an ugly face there, it's yours.

If you see Jesus and Mary, they're you.[20]

When We Are Not Selfless

Acts and words are witnesses of the mind within.

From these two deduce inferences as to the thoughts.[21]

Anything we do contains the same essence and message as *everything* we do. A student of mine was always rushing. She rushed to meet deadlines at work, rushed her food, rushed to the gym, and rushed into love affairs. These actions reveal the mind within, the operating system that guides her behavior. The myth of a person like this, who rushes everything, is one of fear about scarcity—that things will not be there for her if she does not consume them immediately. And, of course, consuming them immediately is exactly what she did, so her affairs never lasted and her life was never calm. By simply slowing down and relaxing, her life became so much richer, and love had a chance to grow.

Another man was very angry and controlling. He would erupt aggressively in public if his coffee was not served to him exactly as he wanted it. On another occasion he almost got himself and a friend arrested when he caused a scene in a restaurant because the water he had asked for didn't have enough bubbles to his liking! And he took instant offense if people did not mention him by name and give him credit for any venture he had been even peripherally involved with. The issue for this man was control. His inner world was so out of control that he tried to stamp it on everyone and everything around him—to his detriment, of course, since he lost a lot of friends that way as people found him erratic and frightening. By not dealing with his inner issues, he lost control of the outside world too, precisely by trying to force his control on others. Eventually, he found himself alone and without friends, and, in this sad way, he gained all the control he needed (and returned to the original issue: himself) because there was no one left to bully.

Loss of power is never entirely one-sided because we must be in agreement in some way with those we allow to take our power that we will accept their definitions of who we are. We must also agree to the rewards we believe they offer us in return for giving up power. There is a form of contract between us: we give ourselves away, they reward us with acceptance, security, belonging, or even with the reinforcement of our victim role, so we can stay in our comfort zones without having to stretch to new possibilities. In the example of the bully above, he may have lost his friends, but at least he gained the illusion of control. After all, when you live in a world of one, you can do anything you like.

In shamanic terms, we give away power because of our "self-importance," which is the opposite of selflessness. When we are self-important, our egos place us at the center of every drama, whether it is positive or negative, good or bad. It doesn't matter, in other words, what role we take—heroes or villains, victims or rescuers—as long as we have a role to play. It is this role-playing that keeps us attached to the people and circumstances that bring us pleasure and pain, distanced from the Beloved and the flow of love in the universe.

This duality and separation into "us and them," "I and That," underlies all dramas that have to do with power. We crave attention from others because that is what we have been taught to do, and so we become addicted to compliments and insults, love affairs and remorse, accomplishments and failures, as a way of proving who we are to ourselves and others. Since there is no absolute indicator of "success" or "failure," however, we are actually in search of the unattainable—because, ultimately, only *we* can know if we are "good" (or "bad") enough; there is no one else who can do this for us.

While we see ourselves as separate from the flow of the universe, we can never be in that flow; while we see ourselves as seekers *after* love, we can never *have* love. As soon as we let go of our self-importance, however, we find ourselves attached to nothing and at one with everything. When we abandon labels and limitations, we allow ourselves at least the possibility of a power that may be immense.

> The fearful ascetic runs on foot, along the surface.
> Lovers move like lightning and wind.
> No contest.
>
> Theologians mumble, rumble-dumble [about] necessity and free will,
> While lover and Beloved
> Pull themselves into each other.[22]

Loving the Tyrant

The rose, though its petals be torn asunder,
Still smiles on, and it is never cast down…
What is Sufism? "Tis to find joy in the heart
Whenever distress and care assail it."[23]

Sometimes, so we can escape our dramatic distractions from truth, the universe sends us a gift in the form of a tyrant who shakes us up until we finally get the message about what is really important.

Petty tyrants, as some traditions call these gifts of the universe, may seem anything but good news when we first encounter them. They are irritants sent to annoy or undermine us. The bully may be an example, or the demanding parent or boss, or those self-important minor officials who smother us in bureaucracy and red tape instead of doing their jobs to make the system work. They are not tyrants on the scale of dictators who cause hurt and distress to millions, and their actions are rarely harmful on a physical level; rather, they needle their way into our minds and emotions, drawing us into their dramas so we are subtly disempowered and our ability to love is challenged.

The main players, as far as tyrants go, are rescuers, persecutors, and victims, and there is a connection between them all, as this schematic shows.

Persecutors

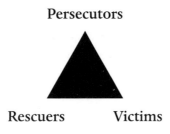

Rescuers   **Victims**

Persecutors

Examples of persecutors include nagging spouses, nitpicking teachers, perfectionist parents who "only want the best for you," and bosses who demand (rather than ask) for more than you are paid to deliver.

They are people for whom nothing is ever right or good enough. Their game is to wear you down, chipping away at your sense of yourself, until you surrender to their rules and do as you're told. Then they can feel self-important, powerful, and more in control of their own lives.

Persecutors are inherently weak and afraid, which is why they try to take power from others. They therefore need victims in order to play their game, and the two are often driven by a common purpose and quite adept at finding each other. Persecutors and victims *need* each other and can switch between roles as well.

The Edward Albee play *Who's Afraid of Virginia Woolf?* depicts a perfectly dysfunctional marriage, with husband and wife swapping roles as attacker and attacked, persecutor and victim, until their final realization that they are playing a game of skewed love for each other to distract themselves from a painful truth: that they are both mourning the loss of their child and will play the abuse game forever until they can weep together. All games like these are distractions in one form or another so we do not have to experience our separation and suffering or to apply ourselves to *zikr*, our remembrance of unity, once more.

Rescuers

Rescuers can sometimes spice up the game of persecutor and victim but are not actually essential to the drama. Where they are drawn into the plot, they can very often be turned on by both sides, who attempt to make them victims too: proof absolute that a game is being played.

The rescuer is the self-sacrificing superhero, ready and able to take on another's battles with no thought for himself. Bravo! Except that, by getting involved in the dramas of others, the rescuer is really doing two things: firstly, he provides himself with an external distraction so he doesn't have to deal with his own inner issues (the need for attention, for example); secondly, by stealing the drama from others and putting himself center-stage, he takes power from both sides at once.

In their archetypal forms as comic book heroes, rescuers are often revealed as little more than vigilantes and even as persecutors themselves, driven by their sense of an injustice done to them. Thus, we have Batman, whose parents were killed by a criminal, who takes revenge against all crime rather than dealing with his own pain of loss.

On the other hand, rescuers also make excellent victims and, on the larger canvas, every body bag that comes home from a war is filled with a rescuer who gave up his life for another.

Rescuers need persecutors, someone to save us from (or at least the myth of persecution). Hence, the "war on terror," with thousands of rescuers deployed into battle against an invisible enemy, without a single "weapon of mass destruction" having been found—in that sense, a victimless (and even a persecutor-less) war, but an engrossing game nonetheless.

Victims

It is perhaps surprising that the greatest tyrants of all are often victims. Persecutors can attack anyone, after all; they do not always need a willing victim. Rescuers can play hero even if their services are not requested or required, but victims need both persecutors and saviors. Whichever role you play (hero or villain), by allowing yourself to be drawn into their drama, you become the victim of the victim who is in control of the game and takes power and attention from both sides.

Victims need rescuers (power from another) because they have not dealt with their own issues of loss or found their own power, and so they take it from others. In order to be "saved" (fed with power), they must therefore also attract persecutors. Then there is always a drama to be saved from and someone to save them from it. In this way, they receive all the attention they need.

Which One Are You?

To understand your own games with power and where you are distracting yourself from the real quest for love, it is helpful to look at the schematic above and ask yourself which role you most often play: victim, rescuer, or persecutor.

There is often a "power loop" involved, so these roles are interconnected. One student, for example, always started off believing he was doing his best for someone he cared about when he intervened as a rescuer to solve a problem for them, but then found he had unwittingly become a persecutor as he tried to impose his solution on them. Finally, he became a victim when he realized that his intervention was not even wanted! Then he would either seethe quietly for a while, waiting for a rescue himself, or get over his anger at rejection and, feeling guilty about his response, go looking for another victim to save! And so the cycle went on. Perhaps you recognize some of this, or another power loop, in yourself?

The rescuer-persecutor-victim cycle is one way we give up our power by becoming embroiled in inauthentic relationships and distracting ourselves from genuine love by involving ourselves in dramas. The solution is to give up the game and take responsibility for our thoughts and actions so we conserve our energy for the journeys to love we must make.

> If you become addicted to looking back
> Half your life will be spent in distraction
> And the other half in regret.
> You can live better than that!
> Find happier friends.
> Say: Show me the faults of my destructive actions
> But don't show me what's wrong with my good work,
> That way I won't get disgusted and quit![24]

When we understand the nature of petty tyrants, we give ourselves a great advantage on our journey, because we discover information about ourselves that we can use for our spiritual transformations. In this way, our tyrants become allies, not enemies, and give us mirrors in which we can see ourselves. Through their efforts they show us our real enemies—those within.

> In the Way of Love, his image is like my guide.
> I speak about the Way, but I keep silent about the guide.[25]

Shamans say that the tyrants we attract into our lives are there for a reason. We feel an affinity with them in some way, and they stand as reflections for ourselves. So, whoever it is that is upsetting you and in whatever way, it is worth asking yourself what buttons they are pushing and whether you recognize their behavior in yourself. The answer is probably yes. This is the tyrant's gift: they allow us to discover new things about ourselves and the circumstances, situations, or people we most often give power to.

Learning to love the "enemy" then becomes a quest to rediscover and embrace those parts of ourselves which we have suppressed or ignored. By so doing, we move closer to spiritual balance; our capacity for tolerance, compassion, and true love grows; and our progress becomes deeper and more rapid as we move toward greater emotional maturity.

Explorations

The following exercises will help you explore the points of this chapter; namely, that:

1. We know little about who we really are. Instead, we select key events from our lives to build our stories around. These stories emerge from our deepest myths of ourselves, which are often informed by other people: our parents firstly, who have unconsciously (or consciously) given us instructions in who we are through their actions and words toward us. They have also passed on some of the energy of their own life dramas, which then become ours—but only for as long as we choose to live them.

2. Through this, our actions in the world are, to some extent, predetermined, and we find ourselves attracted to people who reinforce our scripts and myths. Petty tyrants are an example, but so are those we choose as lovers and friends.

3. While we remain attached to our stories, we will continue to give away power. And yet the truth is staring us in the face every day that our stories are not real. Physically, we are new people each morning when we stand before the mirror. Our bodies are in constant change. We are not our histories, herstories, or stories, period; we are new people each day, and our pasts, presents, and futures are all available to change. There is only ever the infinite Now, and we can choose—if we wish—a life filled with wonder and love.

4. Love is power; power is love. This is the essence and energy of the universe, and it also flows through us. The more we take back our power and use it consciously and with awareness, the more available we make ourselves to love and fulfilment.

The Tyrant's Message

Close your eyes and breathe slowly and deeply. Bring to mind the image of someone who annoys or irritates you, causes conflict or pain in your life, or unbalances you in some other way. Once this image is formed, ask yourself (or it):

- In my relationship with this person, what role do I play (victim, persecutor, or rescuer)?

- What is the power loop involved in this, and how do I feel at the end of it?

- What outcomes do I see in my life as a result of my involvement in this drama?

- In what ways am I exactly the same as this tyrant? What needs and values do we share? What are we both looking for—and not looking at—in our lives?

- What does this drama serve to distract me from?

- If this drama was not in my life, how would I use the energy I expend on it instead?

- Given the myths I carry (see page 72), how does this drama support my self-limitations?

- If I were the tyrant concerned, what would I wish to change in myself?

- What stops me from making this change? What are the risks involved?

- Am I prepared to take these risks? If so, what will change and what will I do instead?

Listen to the advice of your soul, and then, as strange as it may seem, send love to this tyrant. Thank them for the information they have given you and for the power you now have to make changes, which you would not have had if you hadn't met them. You are really sending love and thanks to yourself.

> The eminence you think you want, the power over others,
> Let all that go.
> It's better not to ride on other people's backs;
> That's how we arrive at the grave.
> Tend just to what's yours.
> Breathe out and open your eyes.[26]

The Nature of My Relationships

Loving relationships are another area where we are challenged to learn from each other and to let our stories go.

Whenever we enter a relationship, we stare into a mirror and meet at a level of mutual storytelling. If we allow our egos to win, we will play out our mythological dramas and never really *see* our lovers. The nature of our stories—"I'm the bad guy; save me from myself and teach me how to love" / "I've been hurt by men before; please be the one for me"; "You're all I deserve" / "I deserve better than you," and so on—

become the patterns we repeat unthinkingly instead, without consciously understanding their true implications for us or our lovers. Unless we recognize love as a means to growth, then we fail as love's students and become hooked once again by events from the past. As soon as we decide to take back our power from our stories, though, we give love the freedom to grow, and we see it for what it is: a master class in true loving intent.

Close your eyes, breathe into your heart center, and relax. Call to mind a lover you have shared a drama with. It could have been the love of your life or a total disaster. It doesn't matter which because the real questions are these:

- What story was being played out—for you and for him or her?

- In what ways was the outcome inevitable, given the plot line to this story?

- In what ways could that outcome have been different? What (often subtle things) would have needed to be changed?

- What would the outcome have been then?

- Why didn't you make those changes? Why didn't your lover?

- What has been the cost—to you and to her or him?

- And what has been the payoff—that is, the rewards for acting the way you both did? There is always some reward, even if it is that we remain in our comfort zones and stick with the stories we know (which may be ones of pain and loss, but at least they are familiar).

To take back power from this situation so you do not unconsciously repeat these patterns again, see yourself, eyes still closed, sitting with your lover in an empty room. Notice that strands of energy connect you, and that there may also be a discrepancy in the places where these strands connect (e.g., they may leave your heart but reach your lover's head). This will give you insight into the nature of your respective stories and show where miscommunication is taking place. When you are ready, say whatever needs to said to the person in front of you, so you can forgive or make amends, understand your relationship better, and then end your stories together.

Use your breath to release the energy that ties you to each other. Breathe in to reclaim your power and out to release theirs back to them. Then say your goodbyes, turn around, and walk out of the room you are visualizing, leaving your lover there.

Gently open your eyes and say aloud to yourself, "I am free of that relationship and from that pattern of drama." You can now pursue your truth and leave the stories behind.

A variant of this exercise could also be used for current relationships. By meeting your partner in dreamspace and cutting any unhealthy ties between you to old stories and relationship myths that have grown stale and unfulfilling, you release each other to meet once again in truth and to make a fresh, loving start.

> Don't worry about repenting.
> Do the work that's given
> And learn from it.[27]

The Priest Who Knew Too Little

ONCE UPON A TIME (which, of course, was really no time at all), a mission house stood near a river. The priests at the mission liked to take canoe trips to preach to the people who lived in the villages along the riverbank, to tell them stories about the power and glory of God.

One day, a priest arrived at a village and began to speak. The people listened excitedly and were especially taken with one story, about a man that God had raised from the dead. Pleased with his performance and thinking he had done his job well, the priest finished his story and got back in his canoe to paddle upstream to the next village.

He returned a few days later and was greeted by many jubilant villagers, who ran to hear more of his fabulous tales. Then the village holy man stepped forward. "I want to thank you," he said. "That story you told a few days ago about the man who was brought back from the dead—our chief recently died, so I tried your method on him, and it worked. I am grateful to you."

The priest, in fright, ran back to his canoe and paddled quickly downriver, away from those savages and back to the mission house, where such things do not happen: the dead stay politely dead, and our stories are, well, just stories.[28]

. . .

four

Life Games and Their Players

Finding a Pathway to Love

Of this there is no academic proof in the world;

for it is hidden, and hidden, and hidden.

RUMI[1]

By working on our fears around love (chapter 2: the east, *maqam an-Nafs*) and reconnecting to our power and the spirit of the universe (chapter 3: the south, *maqam-al-Qalb*), our journeys now take us to the west of the medicine wheel and the station of pure spirit (*maqam-ar-Ruh*). The quest we are on now is to find the best and most fulfilling ways of using the courage and power we accept as ours.

Our explorations so far have taught us that there are many responses to life and to love but that our normal reactions may be habitual, limiting, and absorbed from others instead of a truth we have discovered for ourselves. These are inauthentic responses because they do not reflect the true nature of our own loving souls. As we wake up to this fact and move into authenticity, we begin to examine more closely what "being real" means to us and to find new strategies for staying connected to love. This is the work of the west.

> All the world's a stage, and all the men and women merely players:
> They have their exits and their entrances;
> And one man in his time plays many parts.

We might paraphrase this famous line from Shakespeare's *As You Like It* to: "Life, when lived inauthentically, is little more than a game, a series of dramas that we agree to play parts in." Some people would rather play these games or subject themselves to those of others than wake up to reality and understand what we are being asked to do, or what we are asking of others, when we take part in such games. The Sufi mystic Hakim Jami wrote of this when he spoke of the seekers of love that:

> There are plenty: but they are almost all seekers of personal advantage.
> I can find so very few Seekers after Truth.[2]

In psychology, a game is defined as "a recurring set of transactions ... with a concealed motivation ... or gimmick."[3] Our relationships, actions, and interactions are more often *distractions*, that is, designed to elicit a response from others and keep us and them trapped within our habitual roles.

Even if the life game we play ultimately hurts us (as it might, for example, if we push the limits with dangerous games like "drug addict" or "vengeful ex-lover"), it still provides us with a payoff by keeping us safely within our self-limitations so we don't have to stand in our power, take full responsibility for our actions, or do something new and unfamiliar.

Dancing within our personal myths and drawing from the stories we have accepted about ourselves, we play these games of life that prevent us from seeing the truth about who we really are, what we are capable of when we ignite the divine spark within us, and the love that is always ours. Sometimes our games are playful and fun, sometimes hurtful and wounding; sometimes we play nice, and sometimes we cheat; we may win or lose, sometimes nobody wins; but always we play—until the day we decide to break free of our patterns and do something real with our lives.

The Games of Life

Games theory (or transactional analysis, as it also called) was developed by the psychologist Eric Berne as a way of looking at human relationships. A game is a series of subtle cues and communications (in words, gestures, body language, and so on) that make up a pattern or way of presenting ourselves and that therefore lead to familiar interactions with people who are playing on the same field as us because they have a similar reason for being in this game, most likely because their life stories complement ours.

To use our earlier example of tyrants, victims and persecutors play on the same field; one with a desire to be hurt, the other with an interest in hurting. The game between them has a predictable pattern to it:

1. The victim and persecutor are usually *both* aware of the trigger cues, words, or behavior that lead to conflict. Instead of avoiding these triggers, however, either one of them may use one or more of these as cues to provoke a response from the other and begin a new game.

2. In the game of victim and persecutor, the victim gets hurt and may leave the persecutor, but will often return later so the play can resume. This is the pattern in many abusive relationships, for example, which, according to the research, may involve thirty or more such comings, goings, and penitent reunions as the cycle continues and the codependency (a form of obsessive love) between the players grows. When this behavior is recognized as a psychological game that either side may provoke, it is sometimes less easy to see who is the abuser and who is abused.

3. All games lead to a payoff or "goal," as Berne called it—that is, a reward of some kind—for at least one of the players and usually both. The game will thus continue until the costs of playing outweigh the rewards or until there is an injury on the field (an unfair game play that breaks the "rules"). Then play must stop, at least temporarily. In the case of the abusive relationship, for example, "upping the stakes" might mean getting other family members or the police involved while still remaining with the abuser, so that the drama escalates. This is still within the rules since no one has actually called a halt to the play. Breaking the rules might mean leaving the relationship, period,

so the game cannot continue at all. When that happens, there is often pain and shock for both partners as they wake up to the fact that they have been playing instead of taking part in a real relationship. During counseling sessions, an "abuser" will often subsequently say—and really mean this—that he or she didn't even know they were hurting their partner, or knew it and wanted to stop but didn't know how to, while the "abused" may remark that, rationally, he or she can't understand why they remained with their partner so long, but just felt compelled to stay. It is as if they have both been so entranced by the game that they were disconnected from reality.

As in cases like these, the payoffs involved can look odd to someone outside the game because, in fact, the reward can be pain. But pain is what some people know as love.

As an example, I had a student once who was a little difficult and who, through her behavior, seemed intent on trying to get me and the other workshop participants to "beat" her—that is, to put her down, criticize her actions, and get angry with her. There is an expression in some spiritual teachings that we must sometimes "fiercely love" each other. It means that no matter what a person presents to us or how they appear to want us to react, we must fiercely and passionately cling to love. If the way we are invited to respond is out of resonance with love, then in equal measure we must pour more love upon that person and challenge them to learn and to love in response.

One evening, this student acted so inappropriately, I knew she was looking for a "beating." I decided to fiercely love her instead.

In the next workshop session, she had what seemed to be a breakthrough about her life and an insight into her own game. As a child, she had been literally and physically beaten by her mother—"like a dog," she said—and a beating is what she had come to equate with love.

We all believe, as children, that our parents love us and act in our best interests; a beating, therefore, was what this student "knew" love to be. What she had come to realize, however, was that there are other ways for love to be given, and she didn't have to act out scripts or play games in order to ask for it. Once she understood that, she became a delightful member of the group: helpful and kind to others, open and vulnerable with her feelings, and, at the end of the course, one of the best-loved students of all—in a good way. In her case—and in all others—beneath every game we play, there is a search for love and acceptance.

All games end when they are seen for what they are and brought into conscious awareness, because then we can make choices based on knowledge and decide to love honestly instead of letting our life stories rule us and our games leak out.

Identifying our game is the first step. Here are a few that Berne identified from his work with students and clients. Perhaps you will recognize one of these or a variant of it in your own relationships.

If It Weren't for Him …

Berne used this example to explain the principle of games, how they work, and what they aim to achieve. In it, a woman complains that her domineering husband controls her life, to the extent that she never learned to dance despite her desire to take classes. Her husband finally relents, and she signs up for a class that she's always wanted to take—only to find she has a morbid fear of dance floors.

Since she chose this "domineering" man as her husband, what game is actually being played here, asks Berne, and what is the payoff involved?

Actually, there are many payoffs. The woman has fun with her friends, who also just happen to have "domineering husbands," meeting them for coffee to play *If It Weren't for Him* together, where they all complain about their men. Thus, their husbands perform a social function in keeping their circle together and giving them something to talk about.

At the same time, the women never do anything to change their situations or take responsibility for their own lives because their husbands do everything for them. They call this "controlling," but actually it is a useful service. This particular woman's husband, for example, was not only protecting her from something she was deeply afraid of (taking her freedom, represented by dance lessons), but he was even preventing her from becoming aware of her fears (the freedom of the dance floor).

One of Rumi's observations in the *Masnavi* is that "everything is made manifest by its opposite."[4] Thus, in this marriage game, "control" really equals love and protection: positive feelings made manifest by their opposite. The downsides are a marriage in difficulty and a loss of the soul to illusion: playing at love and criticizing the lover instead of truly loving.

Kick Me/Don't Kick Me (Please)!

My student who equated beatings with love was playing a form of this game. According to Berne, it is like wearing a sign that reads "please don't kick me." The temptation is to do so, even though we would never have thought of it if we hadn't seen the sign in the first place.

In this game, the behavior of the person who wears the sign becomes more and more provocative until someone eventually does "kick" them—with a harsh word, a sarcastic remark, or even a physical blow. At this point, they cry "foul" against their "attacker," pointing out that the sign says please *don't* kick me. They can then embark on a new game, such as *Why Does This Always Happen to Me?* This may even have been the real game they were playing all along, with *Don't Kick Me* as a sub-game so they could maneuver themselves into a stronger role.

Once again, what the sign-wearer is looking for is not a kick, but love and belonging. The solution to this game, therefore, is to re-educate the player through genuine love (fiercely given at times) and through compassion, patience, and kindness, so they learn how to ask more effectively for the affection they really need.

As fierce lovers, we also need to ensure that we stand in our own power and give love authentically so we are not playing games as well, such as rescuer or savior. Two Sufi sayings are useful here:[5]

Heart to heart is an essential means of passing on the secrets of the Path, so that we act from genuine love and compassion—from our hearts and not our conditioning—and:

Learning is in activity, so we show people how to love through example rather than lectures, because "learning through words alone is minor activity" and will often involve us in a game we did not intend (such as teacher or guru).

Now I've Got You!

We see this game in many relationships where one person is routinely disempowered by the other and then suddenly and unexpectedly gets their power back again.

Berne's example is of an extremely house-proud woman who constantly attacks her husband for making a mess—perhaps to the extent that she may have a cleanliness compulsion or obsession.

One day, the husband comes home to find that his wife has herself left a mess. "Now I've got you," he thinks to himself as his anger gets the better of him at all the humiliations and criticism he has received from his wife about making just the sort of chaos she has left for him. Instead of breathing a sigh of relief at his wife's more relaxed attitude, he waits for her to get home so he can spend the evening attacking her as she has attacked him.

The saner and more loving solution would have been to nip this game in the bud by using the situation to talk openly and honestly about their marriage so they could make the changes needed, for "sometimes the effect appears before the cause," as the Sufi Abu-Ishak Chishti remarked.[6] Instead, the game is allowed to win and becomes one of empowerment and disempowerment, obsession and revenge, to the detriment of love.

See What You Made Me Do?

According to Berne, this game is a "three-star marriage buster." A man (or woman), wanting a little quiet time, goes off alone on some adventure—maybe just as far as the garden shed, where he gets involved in a carpentry project.

His wife or kids, wanting "strokes" (love and attention from him) but unable to ask for them directly, follow him to the shed on some ruse; for example, to ask where to find something in the house. This interruption startles him and "causes" his saw to slip so his work is ruined, at which point he goes into a rage and shouts, "See what you made me do?" His wife goes away rejected, angry, and perhaps a little ashamed, since her attention-seeking has also been busted. The same sort of scenario is repeated throughout the years, until the wife and kids tend to leave the man alone so they won't get shouted at, and a distance between them grows.

The truth is that it was never the "interruptions" but the man's need for space and his irritation at having it intruded upon which "caused" his various slip-ups. Furthermore, he is delighted when these "accidents" happen, because they justify his desire to be alone ("other people get in the way") and his rage toward unwanted visitors ("see how you ruined my work!").

The saner and more loving solution is for the man to examine his need for solitude and where his relationships require work so he doesn't feel this constant urge to be alone. Instead, he distances himself from the issues by withdrawing from them completely and allowing his relationships to deteriorate.

"Escape the poison of your impulses," Rumi counsels in such situations. "The sky will bow to your beauty if you do."[7]

> Turn away from the cave of your sleeping.
> That way, a thorn expands to a Rose.[8]

Frigid Woman

This is a game played by couples in a long-term sexual relationship. The man makes loving advances to his partner, who opens the game by pushing him away. He tries again and is told, in a somewhat irritated voice, that all he is interested in is sex, that he doesn't love her (or love her enough, or just for herself), that all men only want one thing, or some variant of this. After a few of these rejections, he gives up.

But then something curious happens. His partner starts to become "forgetful." She "forgets" to close the bathroom door when she is showering; she "absent-mindedly" walks around the house half-naked, not for a moment imagining this might have any effect on her partner, who has had no loving contact for weeks. If she is playing a hard game, she may even "forget" that she is married and flirt "innocently" with other men in front of her husband.

Taking the bait, the man makes a move toward his lover and is again rejected. He decides then that he won't fall for the same trick again and now leaves his wife well alone, despite her continuing forgetfulness.

Then, one night, another strange thing happens: she approaches him and nature begins to take its course. Just when things are looking promising, the woman pulls away again with a look of shock and disgust on her face. "See!" she cries. "All men ever want is sex! I just wanted a cuddle, but you just can't keep your hands off me, can you?"

What is it this woman really wants? Not affection, it seems, but attention. And what life story underlies her game? Probably one that comes from mother and begins with "All men are …," or from father and amounts to "You are my princess." Princesses do not have sex; they sweep through fairy-tale landscapes pursued by lovesick and impotent princes. Indeed, if you are daddy's princess, you *can't* have sex with anyone else because that would be disloyal, and you can't have sex with daddy, for obvious reasons. So you have sex with no one, allowing your urges to be satisfied by the attention you get instead.

What would be the saner and more loving solution? To listen to the truth of the body, recognize its needs, and surrender yourself to love.

> A naked man jumps in the river, hornets swarming above him.
> The water is the *zikr*, remembering: There is no reality but God.
> There is only God.

The hornets are his sexual remembering: this woman, that woman.
Or if a woman, this man, that.
The head comes up. They sting.

Breathe water.
Become river head to foot. Hornets leave you alone then.
Even if you're far from the river, they pay no attention.[9]

Let's You and Him Fight

Almost every romantic drama in literature, film, theater, or life follows the format of this game. A woman (or man) finds herself in a situation (or engineers one) where two potential lovers make a play for her affections. She then maneuvers them into fighting for her, with the promise (direct or implied) that she will give herself to the winner. The men fight, and she then either fulfils her side of the bargain or she doesn't, the attention and not the "contract" being what really mattered in the first place.

In this game, it is expected that someone will get hurt. The serious wounding, however (as well as the irony), comes from deciding something as important as love or marriage on the grounds of a fight, which appeals to our basest competitive instincts.

This game always leads to separation, as well, between the woman and the man who "wins" her, since she, through her maneuvers, sets herself apart and above her lover, while he lowers himself to scrabbling round in the dirt for her. Thus, the two can never meet as equals, but only as mistress and servant, the roles often swapping and changing through the years as the man's resentment toward his partner leaks out.

This game most likely originates from a life story on the woman's part of "you are my princess," and on the man's part of "I am not worthy of love in myself (and so I have to earn it)." Western society also encourages such behavior from men and women, and most of its dramatic role models—from Helen of Troy to Bridget Jones, John Wayne to James Bond—have played this game throughout history. It is one of the easiest for the sexes to play and, of course, it creates profound relationship problems; not least that true love and honesty are never present in an affair of this kind, where both partners treat the other as a commodity.

This is how it is when your animal energies, the *nafs,*
    dominate your soul…
It's like someone breaks into your house
And goes to the garden and plants thornbushes.
An ugly humiliation falls over the place.[10]

The sane and more loving response is, as it always ultimately is, to know who you are and what you truly want, and to talk to each other; recognize your real needs and ask for them to be met. They won't be, always; but at least the issue is addressed, love is served, and the reality of your relationship is acknowledged so the potential for hurt is lessened.

In the West of the Wheel

The west of the medicine wheel is characterized by the middle stage of our journeys toward love, and its essential quality is the capacity for self-reflection, using a more mature and experienced mind to engage in more skillful thought. It is through this capacity that we can look back over our lives and become aware of the myths we have been living, the stories we have created, and the games we have been playing. When we do so, we have an opportunity to strip away falsehoods, limiting beliefs, and the comedies and tragedies of our pretenses at love, so we can move closer to *genuine* love and connection.

What we most need now is to find a vision for our lives so we have a road map for the next stage of our adventure, to a place where meaning, passion, and happiness might wait for us. A vision like this is vital if we want to remain emotionally healthy and to know what love really is or could be, yet it is often the one thing lacking in our lives. An opinion poll in France, for example, found that 89 percent of people were desperate for something real to believe in, while a study of nearly 8,000 Americans found that 78 percent needed to find "purpose and meaning to my life."[11]

The Lover's challenge is to find this vision. His reward, if he makes it, is self-belief, clarity, the ability to unravel the mysteries of his life, to know more about himself, and to focus on the things that really matter instead of carrying the dramas of his past onto the pathways of his possible futures.

In other words, he has a choice: to continue his fictions and dramas or to be true to himself so he gives birth to a new and more honestly loving self; to:

> Forget your self-importance.
> Be an invisible guide, like the scent of roses
> That shows where the inner garden is.[12]

Knowing How to Know Truth

ONCE UPON A TIME (which, of course, was really no time at all), there lived a very rich man, with a fine home, a loving wife, and beautiful, healthy children. He had everything a man could ever need. But he was not happy. Something kept him awake at nights, and one day he spoke to his wife of it. "I want to know Truth," he said.

Not wanting to see her husband unhappy, his wife said he must go, then, in search of Truth. With that, the man set off.

For years he wandered on his quest, crossing mountains, deserts, the great oceans and wild places of the Earth, but he found no sign of Truth. Then, one day, on a high mountain peak, lost and in a storm, he came upon a cave.

Entering it to take shelter, he found himself in the darkness staring into the face of a crone. Dressed in rags and tatters, her hair knotted and grey, her body misshapen and dirty, she was ugliness itself, stinking, putrid, and vile.

And yet she spoke with such poetry and wisdom that the man's heart immediately melted and his soul recognized her as Truth. Happy his quest was over, he stayed with her for many years, learning the secrets he had come so far to find.

Then, as the end of his apprenticeship drew near, the man began to realize how much he missed his family and how deep his love for them was. Gathering his few belongings, he sat again at the feet of Truth to offer her his thanks. "It is time for me to leave," he said, "but you have been so good to me. In my homeland I am a rich man, so tell me, how might I reward you? Is there something I can do for you in return for all your kindness?"

Truth thought for a moment, her face ravaged in concentration, and then she answered. "There is one thing," she said. "When you tell people that you have met Truth, tell them I am young and beautiful ..."[13]

. . .

What we consider to be true, by and large, are the things we see with our own eyes. "Knowledge aspires to certainty, and certainty again to sight and ocular evidence," as Rumi writes.[14]

And yet we have been so indoctrinated into the ways and values of the world that we cannot reliably trust even these.

Every memory we have, which we regard as so real and important, is just us making sense of events in this moment, now, and is a combination of previous experience and our beliefs about how things should be (mental habits, in other words). We ignore things that don't fit our ideas so that only "main meanings," rather than specifics, are remembered. You recall the plot of your life—your life script—for example, but not all that has happened to get you where you are now.

We cannot trust our memories, because personal history and social conditioning mean we are never objective on life. Instead, we carve out reality so it makes sense to us and fits what we are familiar with. And, given our propensity to accept the authority of others and the worldviews they impose upon us (as Stanley Milgram found; see chapter 3), even subtle things can change us.

The God in the Hat

ONCE UPON A TIME (which, of course, was really no time at all), there was a mischievous god who decided to have a little fun with human beings. If there was a point to his fun-making at all, it was this: to show people how they so easily fall into the trap of believing things to be true when they are not, and build a drama from this instead of seeking their own meanings and arriving at genuine and personal truths. (I don't think there was a point, though; I think this god just wanted to have fun!)

So he put on an unusual hat—one side painted blue, the other red—and made his way down to Earth.

God found the perfect road; one that ran exactly between two fields where different groups of humans were at work. Then he began to walk the road, doing godlike things. Always hiding his smile, he levitated, turned water to wine, and created feasts out of air that he left at the roadside for both groups to eat.

The people were amazed! They ran to their opposites working the field across the road and began talking excitedly about the miracles of God.

"God has appeared!" they cried. "Did you see how he turned water to wine, walked on the air, and left food for us? Great is this god!"

"Yes!" said the others. "And he was dressed in such finery, too, his red hat shining like the sun!"

"But his hat was blue," said the first group. "You disrespect our god!" At this, both groups fell to fighting before they returned to their fields, no longer speaking to each other.

The mischievous god laughed and, turning around, began to walk the road in the opposite direction so that his blue hat now appeared red, and vice versa.

The people rushed together again. "God has appeared once more!" they cried. "Again he turned water to wine, walked on the air, and left food! Even greater is this god!"

"Yes!" cried the others. "And his blue hat was so regal and fine!"

"No," said the first group, "his hat was now red. Once again you disrespect God!" Both groups fell to fighting once more before they returned to their fields.

The mischievous god was now in fits of laughter. He walked the road a last time in his red and blue hat, but, on reaching its center, now he stood still and faced one field, then the other, so both groups could see his hat in all its glory. Then he disappeared, with a smile on his face, returning to his home.

The people came together again. "God has appeared a third time," they said. "And this time his hat was both red and blue. A powerful god indeed!"

"No!" said the first group. "His hat was not red and blue but blue and red!" Once more, fighting ensued.

The mischievous god, watching from afar, fell about in hysterical laughter as the wine and food and the truths he had brought—his gifts to humankind—lay rotting at the roadside as the people continued their battles, having their own fun in the fields.[x]

· · ·

"Believe not foolish assertions of anyone," writes Rumi, and "do not grieve for what is past,"[15] because there is no assertion that is real, only illusions and judgements. Nor is there a past to grieve for, except the one that we cling to. There is only this single moment in which we may know love.

---

x This is my take on a traditional teaching story recounted by Pema Chodron in her book *The Wisdom of No Escape and the Path of Loving Kindness* (Element Books, 1991).

If there is no truth, if reality is fluid and easily changed according to our views of the world, then nothing has meaning or matters—until we give it meaning, that is, and until we choose that truth.

What this also means—if you choose to see things this way—is that since you do not really have a personal history, you can be anyone you want. You can choose *in this instant* to let go of the past, to find a new vision, and to reinvent yourself so you start living your own truths—the meanings *you* give to the world—and find a path, not of heartache, but of heart. You can always choose to love.

All That We Know

> The gold of your intelligence
> Is scattered over many clippings and bits of wanting.
> Bring them all together in one place.[16]

What we know, we know through our hearts: through the experience of our feelings, not through our senses, which bring us an external world that is itself an illusion. Our senses are open to confusion, distraction, and false interpretation, as our psychologists tell us. We lose ourselves in chattering dramas and games when we focus too much on externals. As Rumi writes, "silence gives answers."[17]

Sufis and shamans understand that this silence—the quiet of the heart and all that it knows of love, compassion, and patience—is the basis for a spiritual life, and that these are more than just words; they are a discipline that allows us to know ourselves and develop a more skillful approach to love.

When the philosopher Descartes wrote his now-famous words *cogito ergo sum*—I think, therefore I am—he was using what we might call "Sufi" or "shamanic thinking." The only thing we can know for sure in this weird world without truth is what we, ourselves, think and feel; our own processes are what matter, not external forms or the conditioned beliefs of others. Love, compassion, and patience therefore become strategies for knowing ourselves and the spirit that gives us life.

Love

Whenever we decide to act in a loving way, we notice, through the feelings it creates in us, a warmth and a comfort as our souls begin to shine. This is because a loving act toward another is also love given to ourselves; there is no separation between us, and the same energy links us. If we observe our feelings as we act with love, we will experience an essential truth: that the divine is within us all.

> The body-senses are wavering and blurry
> But there is a clear fire inside.[18]

Compassion

When we act with compassion—by refusing to make judgements about others or to enter their games and reinforce their stories and myths—we change the dynamic of their lives and nudge them toward love. Thus, compassion toward others is an act of generosity to our own souls too, leading us toward peace and happiness so that love can flow.

> [Lovers] make their loving clearer and clearer.
> No wantings, no anger. In that purity
> They receive and reflect the images of every moment,
> From here, from the stars, from the void.[19]

Patience

Whenever we exercise patience, we remain steadfast in our love—loving fiercely if need be—no matter what dramas are presented to us or how enticing are the games of others. We strengthen our souls. In those moments we also become teachers, a living example others can learn from, because we act in flow with the universe and shine like its beacons of light.

> Give the beautiful ones mirrors
> And let them fall in love with themselves.
> That way they polish their souls
> And rekindle remembering in others.[20]

In every situation, we have a choice to act with love, compassion, and patience or in more habitual and unloving ways that arise from our life stories and the games we have learned. The former is truth, the latter illusion. The former brings joy, acceptance, forgiveness; the latter causes pain to ourselves and to others.

Explorations

Use these exercises to help you explore the points made in this chapter; namely, that:

1. There is no such thing as "the plain truth" or "the facts of the matter." These expressions get thrown at us in life by people who are really expressing subjective *opinions* but couch them in terms that seem conclusive and unquestionable so we are swayed to their point of view and give up our power to them. "The objective truth" is the basis for our legal, political, and educational systems, for example, and the more we accept their viewpoints, the more we give away our power for self-determination and the pursuit of our own morality, love, and truth.

2. Having allowed our power to be taken from us through the myth of "objective truth," many of us develop life games to play out the stories we have been told about ourselves. In this way we follow an inauthentic path toward love and, as a consequence, rarely find the true love we are looking for, only further game-playing at the end of our quest.

3. We can, however, change.

4. If this is beginning to sound a little anarchic, that's because it is. The way of the Lover, the Sufi, and the shaman is about taking power back for ourselves and deciding on our own path with heart, because that is the only real way to find love.

> To the spiritual man, the inner voice is its own evidence
> And needs no other proof. [21]

My Games, My Truth, My Path to Love

The games we play most often reveal the habits we are prone to in our relationships with others, and we may play many games at once, with the same person or with a number of different people. Catching ourselves in these games, we can begin to piece together our stories, and, from this, gain insights into our myths.

In your meditations, ask yourself which games you most often play and who with, or recall a situation you've experienced, which is still meaningful to you, and imagine what role you might have been playing or the role that others have seen in you. What was your payoff in playing these roles? What were they intended to achieve? What was the payoff for the other person involved? Which "field," then, do you meet on?

Putting all of your games together, what story do they mesh with in your life? If you saw someone behaving in the same way, that is, what would you decide about who they were, the past they have lived through, and the nature of their dramas? Are they "comedians," "tragic lovers," or "heroic failures," for example? And, from this, what would be the myth that underlies their/your story and their/your interactions in the world?

Giving Up the Games

When we act from habit and play out our stories, we cannot respond authentically to each unique situation and person we meet because our minds, rather than being skillful in our interactions, are, in fact, unused and asleep. It is good, therefore, to willfully break our habits from time to time, to wake ourselves up so we keep to the path of love.

Breaking with habits can change the dynamic of our lives because it involves us in living and seeing each second as a singular moment of choice and power, instead of stumbling unconsciously through our repertoire of dramas. In this way, we are present in our lives and experience them for what they are and for what we choose to make of them.

One way of doing this is to write out your daily routine (if you have a daily routine: this already implies that your time, and so your experiences, are constrained by habit), then make subtle changes to it, and see how this alters the bigger picture. Choose a different route to work, go to a different place for lunch, take up a new hobby in the evenings.

Small changes create dramatic shifts in our lives. They mean we are actively involved in the world. Our bodies feel different as new muscles get used, our emotions are heightened through new experiences, our minds are expanded, and our souls feel attended and fed. Note how the world changes for you. And remember to break these new routines after a while, too, so change does not become a habit in itself.

The Truth of Your Soul

Close your eyes and breathe into your heart. Notice, through your mind's eye, that there is a part of you that is pure consciousness. Observe yourself as this spiritual essence at a time before you were even conceived, a time when you were still part of the pool of conscious energy that suffuses the universe. Explore that feeling of connection for a while, and then see yourself moving forward in time to the moment when your soul made a choice to take human form. You had a reason for this, an intention that was the mission of your soul, your purpose in being.

What did you come here to do, and what gifts and abilities did you bring with you for achieving this? What burdens or handicaps did you also give yourself so you would learn something new from this trip? When you have your answers, breathe out, and open your eyes. Without thinking, and still from a place of feeling, write them down.

Close your eyes again, and observe in your imagination your soul beginning its journey from energy to human form and then entering your mother's womb. See yourself growing there, being born, and living your life through all the key stages you remember, up to your current age. At every stage in this journey, keep your soul-purpose firmly in mind. In this way, you begin to repattern your life and your responses to it.

If there is a body movement that goes with this repatterning—a gesture, a mudra, or a sound—give voice or expression to it, so your body understands your spiritual intention.

Take a few more breaths and allow love, patience, and compassion to fill your heart; feel love toward yourself and toward all those people who have played a part in your life. Even if they hurt you in some way, they have helped your soul to grow because, for one thing, you would not be here without them, exploring your truth, so you can make new choices about your future. Even tyrants bring us gifts of understanding.

Ask yourself: "What do I need to do now so I am true to my reason for being?" What arises in response to this question may be a feeling, a mood, or simply a "knowing," but try to apply an air of practicality to it so you can arrive at a list of actions that will move you closer to your aims. This is the formulation of your vision.

When you are ready, open your eyes and write down this list. Then do whatever needs to be done to get things moving.

Communicating Love More Effectively

How do we act from love and avoid playing games when our patience and compassion is tested, such as during an argument with our lovers? There are no better training grounds than everyday relationships for us to practice our skills of love. The art of loving communication is central to this and requires only your discipline and clarity.

Any interaction can be separated into three components: the data itself, the emotions it stirs within us, and the judgements we make as a consequence. Take the sentence "I hate you for what you've done to me," which is used frequently in one form or another during conflict situations.

First, there is the data. This is simply what was done. For example, Person A (John) forgot his agreement with Person B (Jane) to be at a certain place at a certain time, and this has led to problems for Jane. John's forgetfulness creates an emotional response in Jane, most likely a feeling of rejection or betrayal, causing her to make judgements about John, which will be along the lines of "only a jerk/sadist/monster would behave in such a way, therefore you are a jerk/sadist/monster" and "I hate you for what you've done to me."

It looks simple and obvious enough, but note that stages two and three—the emotions and judgements—actually have nothing to do with John. All he has done is forget something. The rest is Jane's response to that data, which reveals the game she is playing (most likely a form of *Why Does This Always Happen to Me?*), her life story that prompts it (*I'm Not Worth It*), and the myth of self that it stems from (*I Don't Deserve It*). Separating these responses from the data enables conflict to be averted by dealing with the facts, not the dramas they evoke.

Of course, John's motivations for forgetting are not clear from the data, and it could be that he is complicit in Jane's game or playing one of his own in order to maneuver her into the emotional response she makes, but no attempt is made to clarify this; rather, Jane assumes that her lover's actions are deliberate, manipulative, and performed with the intent to hurt her. A simple question ("Why did you forget our agreement?") would enable further data to be drawn out so this could be cleared up between them.

The process is a simple one, but it is not often followed in daily life because, of course, it doesn't allow for dramas to be acted out and life games to be played; it is just a boring exchange of facts between individuals who wish to resolve their conflicts. As each individual notes their internal processes, however, they learn more about themselves and gain control over their emotional arisings, which moves them closer to peace. It's not a very exciting process, but it allows more than anything for love to be given a voice and to flourish, which the alternative will never do. As Sufis say, "at a certain time, more can be conveyed by distracting useless attention than by attracting it."[22]

A good practice in conflict situations is therefore to listen—with your full attention—to what is said in the aim of arriving at pure data, and to resist the temptation
to react or to judge until all the information is in. Then verify the data by asking any
questions you need to about what you have heard in order to clarify things, so you can
respond to facts, not assumptions. Note your emotions as they arise, but don't respond
from them.

As a spiritual practice, try this approach in your interactions with others, whether in
a conflict situation or not, and notice how empathy and communication between you
improves and how your love remains free to flow.

Building Compassion

To use the mind skillfully in the pursuit of love, begin to observe the workings of
your mind. One way to do this is to keep a journal of your emotions for a period of
time (say, three months) and note how you feel in certain situations or according to
certain behavior patterns.

Whenever you act in a way you believe to be loving or unloving, compassionate or
uncompassionate, patient or impatient, note those occasions and how you feel as a
consequence, so you start to explore your inner states. At the end of this time, look for
the common themes that emerge. These will give you insights into the situations and
circumstances in which your love and compassion is challenged, or in which you find it
easier to give love. You then have a choice: to put yourself in the latter situations more
often so that your love can grow, or, if you wish to stretch yourself, knowing what you
find most challenging, to put yourself in these situations as a willful act of love.

Note also, at the end of this period, the simple truth that emerges: whenever you act
lovingly and with patience and compassion, you feel better, lighter, and more radiant,
because your soul is fed by your actions.

As the poet John Keats wrote, "I am certain of nothing but the holiness of the heart's
affections and the truth of imagination. What the imagination seizes as beauty must
be truth."

five

Staying Awake on the Path

Avoiding That "Is It All Worth It?" Feeling

The breeze at dawn has secrets for you:

don't go back to sleep.

RUMI[1]

And so we arrive at the north of the medicine wheel, the station of divine secrets, the *maqam-as-Sirr*. If we have been practicing our love skillfully as we have worked through the three other stations so far, we already know something of our life myths, the stories that compel us, and the games we may have been playing as a consequence of these. We also have some strategies for dealing with such distractions, so we are more authentic Lovers.

The station of *maqam-as-Sirr* is that place in our journey when we must gather our courage, our powers, and our vision so we can apply these insights and talents in order to continue our journeys.

Through our work so far, we know more about our needs, our conditioning, and about love as a divine force, and we are more able to relate honestly and with compassion, patience, and understanding toward others: to see people clearly and to accept them for who they are. But there may still come a time when love seems uncertain or distant. This feeling is like a tiredness, a fatigue of the soul, where the temptation is to disavow the awakening we have had and "go back to sleep"—to ask ourselves if it is all worth it.

The reason for this fatigue is the realization that while we live in this world of forms, trying to find our way back to God and to truly remember ourselves as aspects of that divinity, some part of us will always be separate. Most people have been socialized into a world of pain and conflict, and are not yet awake themselves. They believe so absolutely in a reality of suffering that they do not see an alternative to it. People who speak of love, compassion, patience, and connection in this frenzied and hostile world just seem crazy to them.

"Where is this love you speak of?" they will ask, and you will, of course, be hard put to show them. What can you point to, after all, that demonstrates this love behind the conflicts that are all too obvious? Our responsibility to love is immense, and yet there are no words we can offer to prove that love is real in a world that so often demonstrates its opposite. Rumi writes:

> Whenever the Secrets of Perceptions are taught to anyone
> His lips are sewn against the speaking of the Consciousness.[2]

"Words do not convey the message by themselves … intellect is hampering, and learning is stupidity," as the Sufi mystic Hakim Jami also wrote.[3]

Thus, you become an outsider.

Perhaps it is better to be content with that; outsiders are, after all, the great pioneers of history, to whom we owe most of our progress in all walks of life. But there may also be times when you want to be "inside," and you will therefore find yourself putting effort and energy into explaining, time and again, the unexplainable—the mysteries of love and truth—to people who cannot hear them.

> God created pain for this purpose …
> To manifest happiness by its opposites.[4]

But If Not Love, Then What?

In fact, everyone does know, at a deep soul level, that there is more to life than suffering and the routines they adopt to distract themselves from it. They just don't know what it is. The psychiatrist Viktor Frankl wrote of a survey among European students where 25 percent were going through what he called an "existential vacuum," or lack of meaning, in their lives. Among Americans it was 60 percent. "The existential vacuum manifests mainly in a state of boredom [which is] now causing, and certainly bringing to psychiatrists, more problems to solve than distress," he said.[5]

Frankl used the example of "Sunday neurosis," that kind of depression that afflicts people who become aware of the lack of content in their lives when the rush of the busy week is over and the void within themselves becomes manifest.

His conclusion was that underlying our daily routines there is emptiness. Our routines and the reality they are there to prop up are both illusions, and when people's time, energy, and ability to think is not taken up with work commitments and chores, they become all too aware of this. For those who do not discover a spiritual love to fill this vacuum—or at least, as you have done, begin their journeys toward it—life itself becomes meaningless. The temptation for many is to run from this emptiness—to turn away from the challenge of the east, which is to face their fears—and to fill the gaps of meaning in their lives with new distractions. In doing so, they settle for the majority view of a world built on separation and anxiety, and thus they give up on love entirely.

Overcoming this fatigue is the Lover's challenge, so that we might find the laughter and silence of mature spirituality and wisdom, which is "not of earth, not of water, not of air, not of fire; not of throne, not of ground, [but] of existence, of being."[6]

The thirteenth-century Sufi Saadi wrote of this challenge when he related a dream he had where he saw a dervish (an enlightened soul) in hell, while a king who had devoted his life to power and riches sat in heaven. He wondered how this could be, since surely their positions should be reversed. Why would the dervish be in hell after his devotion to love and a spiritual life, while the king, who cared only for wealth, sat in paradise? As he asked this question, a voice answered him: "The king is in heaven because he respected dervishes. The dervish is in hell because he compromised with kings."[7]

If we remain true to our spirit and do not lose ourselves to the illusions of the world—fame, status, power, wealth, celebrity, and other kingly deceits—then we can avoid pain. But if we "compromise with kings," we are lost.

The aim of the Lover, therefore, is to retain (or, rather, to rediscover) the purity of spirit, balance, and connection he first knew as a child. He can then use his gifts of courage, power, and clarity with continued trust and vitality. But if he gives away his energy to kings, he gives away his soul and opens himself to fatigue.

All of this is the work of the north, which, on the medicine wheel, is about staying true to our vision so we bring spirit into matter and relate to the heart and soul of the physical world, not just its material form.

In order to do so, the Lover must embrace his fatigue as an ally, understanding that every time he is tired of life or wounded by love he has a chance to look more closely at who this tired and wounded person is and what changes he needs to make to ensure that his soul is fed. The message from fatigue, in fact, is to remain on the path, because you are about to enter a new understanding: that joy and pain are both just labels, not the truth of anything; that reality is flowing and changes second-by-second as we navigate the infinite moment.

"The clear consciousness-core of your being [is] the same in ecstasy as in self-hating fatigue," Rumi reminds us.[8] Therefore …

> Be empty of worrying.
> Think of who created thought!
> Move outside the tangle of fear-thinking.
> Live in silence.[9]

For:

> Only sweet-voiced birds are imprisoned.[xi]
> Owls are not kept in cages.[xii,10]

Our job as Lovers, in the north of the wheel, is to stay free and uncaged.

---

xi   That is, those that allow themselves to be treated as commodities.

xii   Owls embody freedom and wisdom.

The Value in Suffering

When it comes to fatigue, our tendency may be to push our pains away and to sublimate or ignore them, but if there is a meaning and value in life, there must also be a meaning and value in suffering, for this too is a part of our human experience. When we recognize this, rather than hiding from our pains and sorrows, we can choose, if we wish, to accept their lessons instead of resisting them and adding to our pain by fighting not to suffer. When we accept the reality of our lives in this way, we learn from our fatigue so it becomes a friend in our quest for love. We may then find that even negative situations have positive gifts to impart.

There are many ways to use our suffering skillfully. The most important and fundamental is to accept our pains with dignity instead of concealing them, ignoring them, feeling ashamed of them, or wishing for something else. If we do that, we will not lose sight of who we are in the fullest of our beings but come to see our suffering as part of our humanity. By working with our shadows in this way, we love ourselves more, instead of denying a part of our souls.

While our wounds remain unconscious, however, we will always be in a place of hidden sorrow and carry our hurts into every relationship, where they will leak out in our actions, our words, and our games, and so cause damage to others. In turn, this damages us more.

Or we may enter relationships looking for salvation from pain—a lover who can save us from the past and heal the "fatal wounds" that others have left us with. This is not authentic love but manipulation. In such circumstances, we are taking the affection of others under false pretenses, knowing in our souls that we are not truly loved for who we are, but only as the thieves of love.

The Sufi philosopher El-Ghazali wrote of this that "if one loves someone because it gives [us] pleasure [or comfort from pain], one should not be regarded as loving that person at all."[11] Instead we are using them.

The aim of true love is to enter a state of union with our lovers, because "love becomes perfect only when it transcends itself—becoming One with its object; producing unity of being," as another Sufi writer, Hakim Jami, described it.[12] This is pure love, which is not predicated on pain or our attempts to escape it.

We see examples of many people who have turned their suffering into power—such as Gill Hicks, who lost both of her legs in the July 7, 2005, London Underground bombings, when an explosive-laden rucksack detonated close to where she was standing, and twenty-six people around her were killed.

Gill spent months in the hospital, going through surgery, having artificial limbs fitted, learning how to walk again, and battling depression at the loss of her previous life.

In an interview with BBC News after her ordeal, however, Gill had no intentions of self-pity. "I feel the overwhelming euphoria of being alive," she said. "How wonderful that I'm here." [xiii]

She has gone on to become an inspiration to many. Rather than seeking revenge for the crimes against her or allowing hatred to consume her, she is now an ambassador for a peace organization. In May 2006, while presenting an award for television current affairs at the BAFTA (British Academy of Film and Television Awards)—the UK equivalent of the Golden Globes—she spoke again about what she called her "second life."

"When something like that happens, you realize what's important: Take a breath. Live your life. Make a difference."

Gill could easily have become trapped by her tragedy, but she chose freedom and love—the desire to "make a difference"—instead. When we do not use our suffering to *maintain* our suffering by looking for sympathy instead of knowledge and power, or trying to distract ourselves from it, like Gill we can use it to enrich our lives.

Wisdom is not to wallow in pain or avoid it, but to flow with it, explore its depths and richness, and accept it as ours, because then we take responsibility for our lives and live them fully instead of putting our energies into illusion: the embrace of pain or the avoidance of the life that we have.

Looked at from a still more philosophical perspective, actually there is no pain in and of itself; not at an emotional level, not even at a physical level (which is why we can sometimes cut ourselves or break bones without noticing any discomfort until we see the blood and assume that we must hurt). It is our *attachments* to things, people, and expectations that create the pains we feel. If we can only let go and find that place where expectations and the labels of "pain" and "joy" do not exist, however, so that

---

xiii   You can read her interview here: http://news.bbc.co.uk/1/hi/uk/4346812.stm (accessed 19 July 2007).

things just *are*, we will remain at one with the natural flow of the universe, and, in this bigger picture, experience not sorrow or suffering, but Life.

The most healing thing we can do for ourselves and others, therefore, is simply to relax and breathe. "Take a breath. Live your life. Make a difference." Slow down so we move at the pace of nature, and learn gratitude and acceptance for the way things are, no matter how they are.

Even if we cannot see the big picture, the cosmic overplay of our lives, it is still better for our souls to trust in love than in labels. Then we do not add to our pains by living only our sorrows in a world which we imagine as loveless. Instead, we learn valuable lessons on the path to a greater love. These lessons may be simple, as the psychologist Dina Glouberman writes, but they can be profound in teaching us how to live in a better and more fulfilling way:

> When you are hopeless, give up hope.
> When you are humiliated, let go of pride and choose humility.
> When you are disillusioned, de-illusion.
> When you are holding on to what you know, let go
>   and surrender to what is about to become.[13]

In these ways we heal, and in these ways we can love. Holding on to our expectations and old dreams in the face of a new reality, and trying to control our lives in a rigid and inflexible way, meanwhile, will inevitably lead to fatigue, because we are putting our energies into an ultimately futile pursuit. The universe is bigger than us and steeped in mystery; asking it to revolve around us and our individual needs is absurd. What we *can* do is trust that it means us no harm, that there is a wisdom to the experiences it grants us, and that we will grow from them: to fiercely love the universe, that is, even when nothing seems to be going our way. This is an act of the greatest faith, but by making it, and by accepting the way things are, we will find that our love and trust is answered.

This letting go—choosing humility and replacing hope with faith, illusion with love—is also a form of remembering what is important: who we are, how the world works, and our true purpose in life, instead of battling to maintain who we *think* we are and how our lives *should* be.

Scars

ONCE UPON A TIME (which, of course, was really no time at all), on a hot summer's day, a little boy decided to go for a swim in the lake behind his house. So delighted was he to be at play in the cool waters that he did not notice, as he swam toward the middle, that an alligator was swimming toward him.

The boy's father saw, though. Working in his yard, he looked up and saw the two as they got closer together.

Dropping his tools, he ran toward the water, yelling to his son to get out. Hearing his father's voice, the little boy became scared and began to swim for the shore. But it was too late. Just as he reached his father, the alligator reached him.

On the shore, the father grabbed his son by the arms as the alligator dug his teeth into the boy's legs, and a tug-of-war began between the two. The alligator was much stronger than the father, but the father was too consumed with passion and the love of his son to let go.

At that moment, a farmer happened to drive by, and, hearing the screams, raced from his truck, took aim with his gun, and shot the alligator.

The little boy survived, although his legs were very scarred from the alligator attack, and his arms, too, were deeply scratched where his father's fingernails had dug into them as he clung desperately to his son.

A newspaper reporter came to interview the boy and asked if he could see the scars. The boy lifted his legs, wincing at the pain.

Then, with obvious pride, he rolled up his shirt sleeves and said to the reporter, "But look at my arms! I have great scars on my arms! I have them because my dad loves me and wouldn't let go."

Some scars are caused by pain, but some are beautiful and there as a mark of love.[xiv]

. . .

---

xiv   Adapted from personal communication.

The Compassionate Soul

There is another reason why fatigue can be a friend to us: it offers a place where all souls meet. The word *compassion* means "suffering with." We are all wounded, and our spiritual wounds all stem from one source: our separation from the divine and our aloneness as a consequence. Layers of hurt may be heaped upon this over the years, but the foundation for our pain is that we are lost to the Beloved, and we want to return to those arms. Our wounds are the marks we wear to remind us of this fact.

Archbishop Desmond Tutu defines compassionate love as "feeling *with* someone, rather than just *for* them … it comes from the desire to try to do something to change the situation that invoked your compassion in the first place … You are *moved* by your compassion. It must impel you to do something to try to change the situation." [14]

Through compassion, "you realize that spirituality is not a lonely journey. It is about growing in a relationship with a community. You then realize that your own humanity depends on that of the other … You cannot be human in isolation … You are human precisely because of relationships: you are a relational being or you are nothing. I am because you are."

We are all connected. Through your recognition of my suffering and your compassion toward me, we are both healed and the space between us is closed. Then we can meet as equals, both of us divine, and reclaim our relationships to the Beloved. Says Tutu: "All that is good in us is a reflection of the divine. As we grow in intimacy with God and so become more Godlike ourselves, we will begin to reflect those attributes."

Part of the Archbishop's work is to bring together victims and persecutors—those who have suffered from violent crimes and those who have caused their suffering—so they can talk about their mutual pain. At these reconciliations, something remarkable happens. When one man spoke of his violent and lonely upbringing in a deprived Irish home, "the victim said that if he had been brought up in the circumstances in which the perpetrator had been, he was certain he too would have done what this guy did. It's about trying to get someone to understand how the other turned out to be who they are." When we meet in suffering and compassion, we begin to understand.

This is not just a spiritual phenomenon. Psychologists who have studied relationships also find that those which endure are based on compassion and what we might call "soul love" rather than just romance. John Gottman has studied relationships for more than thirty years and says that the "masters of relationships"—the people who succeed—have certain features in common:

"For couples whose relationships lasted, the ratio of positive to negative statements during a conflict conversation was five to one. For those in relationships that fell apart, the ratio was about one to one ... It is about being interested in your partner and being receptive and knowing them, and taking in something deep and fundamental about them. It is a moment-to-moment decision to be interested, to be complimentary ... for things to say 'thank you' about. At the other extreme, the 'disasters of relationships' focus on their partner's mistakes. They are scanning for what their partner is doing wrong."[15]

According to Gottman, there are four things that are more corrosive than anything else to loving relationships:

- A superior attitude: insults, sarcasm, and contempt for our lovers in the belief that we are better than they are

- Criticism: finding mistakes and things to complain about in everything our lovers do

- Defensiveness: the belief that we are right in all things or an innocent victim of circumstances and the problem wasn't caused by us

- Stonewalling: where one person simply doesn't respond anymore to their partner

Looking at this list, we can probably simplify it to just this: a desire to remain separate leads to separation; compassion, on the other hand, leads to unity, as we share our truths and focus on the thing that connects us: *love.*

This demands honesty, openness, and a willingness to be vulnerable and to let go of our ego games. Rumi enjoins us to:

> Come down from the pear tree that's been making you dizzy;
> The pear tree of ego and jealousy.
> The pear tree itself will change because of your climbing down.[16]

Better relationships are in this way made, and the search for love and truth is better served.

The Beauty of Death

This invisible ocean has given you such abundance,
But still you call it "death"...
How strange your fear of death and emptiness is,
And how perverse the attachment to what you want.[17]

There is something else that unites us too; one many of us spend our lives trying to avoid: the knowledge of our deaths.

Western culture is so afraid of death that it cannot even say its name. One of the funniest television advertisements I ever saw was for a life assurance company. (Note the name: life *assurance*, not *insurance*, as if they can guarantee immortality through their policies.) It encouraged viewers to buy its products with an appeal to their deepest fears. "How will your wife and family cope," it asked, "if the worst should ever happen?"

I love that phrase: "If the worst should ever happen."

If (Is there any "if" about death?)

The worst ("The worst" is, presumably, my death, but a "life assurance" company cannot admit to death.)

Should ever (You mean I might not die if I buy your products?)

Happen (It *will* happen; I think that's pretty inevitable).

Using a similar strategy, cosmetics companies sell their products by warning us to "keep young and beautiful—if you want to be loved," the implication being that age is not beautiful, and once we are out of our teens (or the façade of youth their cosmetics provide), we are no longer lovable but can look forward only to a few remaining years of decline, followed by nonexistence. Fear and death go hand in hand.

And yet, if we avoid the knowledge of death, we cannot fully live either. Believing that there will always be a tomorrow, we do not make the most of the opportunities life offers today. Nor do we prioritize our time or put our energies to good use; we squander them instead in games and dramas and lose ourselves to fatigue, when the only worthwhile action in the face of death is to love and be loved. Just before those planes hit the Twin Towers, a number of phone calls were made and texts sent by the passengers onboard. Every one of them, as far as it has been reported, had to do with love and farewells. There is no room for games at such times.

Knowing that we will all die one day puts our lives and problems into perspective. When we accept that death is near, the struggle to compete, to win, and to "get one over" on others becomes futile. Do we really believe that "victory" (in someone else's terms or even in our own) is more important than love, or that there is a point to our dramas and conflicts? Conflicts and competitions are the sons and daughters of the illusory world, where we are captives to social reality, but they are never the truth of the world. After all, we cannot take our power and prestige, our wealth and our status, our designer suits or our "victories" over others with us into the next life; we must all travel light, taking only our souls and what we have learned of love.

The practice of reminding themselves of their mortality is known to shamans, in the words of Carlos Castaneda, as "keeping death as an advisor"[18] so we re-engage with the magic and immediacy of life. In this way, fatigue does not overwhelm us, and we can concentrate our efforts on the things that really matter—the mission and perfection of our souls.

The Japanese swordsman Miyamoto Musashi, who faced the possibility of death every day, also wrote of this. "To die with your intention unrealized is to die uselessly," he said. "Consider yourself a dead body, thus becoming one with the way of the warrior, [and] you can pass through life with no possibility of failure."[19]

One of the most profound yet everyday means of retaining death as an advisor is simply to pause momentarily before any action, especially in situations of conflict, and imagine yourself already dead and living your life for the second time; then ask yourself: "Knowing what I know now—that love is the greatest power of all, and little else truly matters—would I still say the same things or act in the same way?"

This is not only a reminder to ourselves to behave with compassion and love, but it is a protection for our souls, since every action we take, every word we speak, and every thought we allow ourselves carries power and has consequences that can be wide-ranging and long-lasting, even though they seem trivial at the time. A moment of reflection and a willful decision to love can save us from fatigue and the expense of a vast amount of energy by preventing conflicts and sparing our souls from guilt, shame, and retaliation. When we make our decisions conscious acts of power instead of unconscious or fearful reactions, we take responsibility for ourselves and avoid the problems which may otherwise come back to haunt us.

Rumi writes of the value of keeping death as an advisor in his parable of "The Deadly Mosque."[20] There was once a haunted mosque, he says, in which "none could sleep a night and live." When, one day, a stranger came to the town and wished to sleep there, the frightened townspeople warned him against it. But the stranger replied that he did not fear for his life, because "the life of the body was naught, and God has said, 'Wish for death if you are sincere' ... The terrors of death did not appall him." And so he entered the mosque.

At midnight he was awakened by a terrible voice and thought himself about to be attacked. Then, pausing to gather his wits, the stranger asked calmly that his unseen foe show himself. "At these words the spell was dissipated, and showers of gold fell on all sides." The stranger left the mosque a hero, richer for his encounter with death.

No matter how bad life seems, how tired and unhappy it makes us, or how afraid we are, whenever we calmly confront our fatigue, we remember what a gift life is: by living it fully and giving ourselves to love, we can change, evolve, and grow so we become heroes to ourselves and divine guides to others.

Living with Patience and Good Intentions

Another way to make sense of fatigue is to use it to hone our intentions, so we give ourselves a focus for our actions and do not expend energy needlessly.

Intention is holding a thought of how our lives will be and then releasing it to the universe, while living as if our vision were already true. If you dream of a more loving relationship with your partner, for example, make this dream as real and as solid as you can, so you see, with total clarity, how life would be if you had this loving relationship. Then live the dream, behaving as if it were already true.

This, too, is acting with compassion, because no matter what difficulties you and your partner are experiencing, your new way of behaving brings both of you closer through your intention to love and understand. When you act kindly and compassionately, no matter what their initial response, your lover cannot help but learn from you and become more loving themselves. It may take time, of course, because they (just as you) will need to unlearn their relationship habits so they trust this new way of being, but it will happen. There is a virtue, therefore, in patience and in dedication to your own loving purpose.

There is no need to hold your vision in a vicelike grip, however. One of the most important spiritual practices we can, indeed, perform to benefit ourselves and others is simply to relax. When we do that, the universe is free to help us, and we do not put up blocks against the flow of love. Instead of rigid thinking, therefore, remain aware of your intention so it acts as a reminder to yourself, but don't let it limit you so you miss the opportunities life sends that fit your loving objectives.

When we believe and trust that things will go our way, rather than forcing the circumstances of our lives to fit around our needs, we find that good things start to happen for us—not always in the way we thought they would, but in the right way for us, if we let them.

Nothing Matters

The Yaqui shaman don Juan had a further word to add about intention. "My acts are sincere," he said, "but they are only the acts of an actor because … nothing matters."[21] This notion of sincere and heartfelt intention combined with the understanding that, in this world of forms, nothing we do is really that important, is known as "controlled folly."

The *Concise Oxford Dictionary* defines a folly as a "foolish act, idea, or practice; a ridiculous thing." Everything we do in life is an act of folly when we make it important, because then we become identified with the things we desire and limit ourselves to specifics instead of embracing the vastness of our beings. We take an agenda into our relationships instead of being present in them.

In a sense, all things are meaningless, but by virtue of being human we must do something. We are material beings in a material world, and our lives are what we have to explore and express our love. There is nothing wrong, therefore, in our desire for certain things or in the meanings we attach to them, as long as we remain aware of their real value as temporary comforts in this life and learning opportunities for the next. In this way, we do not give up our souls to illusion and waste our energies on the ultimately meaningless.

However, when we pretend, for example, that we are important people with needs that must be met, it may well be that, through the power of our intention, we do become important in financial, social, or even relationship terms as our lovers scurry around after us tending to our every need. But these roles that we play are not really us (or all that we are), and a love based on servitude is not authentic love. Self-importance is only ever-transient in the scheme of things.

> All this is the décor of love, the branches and leaves and blossoms.
> You must live at the root to be a True Lover...
> You've done the outward acts but you haven't died.
> You must die.[22]

When we believe in our image and lose ourselves to self-importance, we give up our energy to folly and to prove to ourselves that we really are this important person we believe ourselves to be. At this point, we invite fatigue. It is inevitable.

When we control our follies, on the other hand, and they do not control us, we can follow our own path of truth, with clarity, compassion, and good intentions.

> When he heard that, he lay back on the ground laughing, and died.
> He opened like a rose that drops to the ground and died laughing.
> That laughter was his freedom, and his gift to the Eternal.[23]

Explorations

Through these exercises, you can explore the points made in this chapter. Here, the key points are:

1. That fatigue is a challenge to our spirit. It is caused by the world impinging on our dedication to love and the truth we know in our hearts, through a circumstance that upsets us and creates doubt in our souls.

2. It can look, at the time, as if giving in to fatigue is the most comfortable and easy option; that if we simply *react* to it (for example, by finding a new lover, or job, or interest, to replace the ones we have lost)—doing anything we can to make our suffering go away—then things would get better for us. But this is not truly *listening* to fatigue, which may offer a more positive and creative solution if we open ourselves to its message. Thus, suffering, fully embraced, can be one of the most powerful ways of developing compassion and connection with others, allowing our souls to deepen further into love. If, on the other hand, we simply react or resign ourselves to fatigue, we may do even greater harm by being drawn back into life's dramas, from which we must then start again to free ourselves.

3. Looked at in this way, fatigue can be a gift, because whenever we feel its presence, we are given insight into ourselves and new opportunities to explore love and compassion, to understand who we are and why this pain is afflicting us, and to learn from it so we develop new strategies to be true to ourselves. In this way, we become the masters of fatigue, not in service to it.

4. Fatigue is a friend—in Sufi terms, a guide or a teacher who loves us—not an enemy to love.

The Vision Quest

Many spiritual traditions, such as Sufism, use a form of sensory deprivation to heal the soul and to develop a greater awareness of, and appreciation for, life and the natural world. One parallel shamanic practice is the vision quest, where the seeker goes alone into the wilderness for some days and nights to explore his soul and ask questions of the earth. This strengthens and protects the spirit and helps the initiate to appreciate how beautiful life is, no matter if his experiences are ones of "joy" or "pain."

"Joy" and "pain" are labels we apply to experience, whereas there is something in nature that defies description and links us to the indescribable: the greater soul of the universe, the Beloved.

In the vision quest, the initiate walks out into nature to find a place where he will not be disturbed for a period of time—whether for hours (in the form of a night vigil) or days—and commits to staying there, no matter what. He has specific questions in mind when he does so: "Where have I come from?" and "Where should my life take me now?" Finding the answers to these questions, he is able to order his life and give it direction, purpose, and vision, so his energy is preserved and can be used more effectively.

On the quest, he will sit quietly, observing nature for the answers, in the knowledge that it is alive and talking to him and will provide the information he needs. The shape of a cloud, the flight of a bird, the song of the breeze in the trees—are all omens and signs, if he lets them speak to his soul.

> O you who are a copy of the divine Book,
> You who are a mirror of the royal beauty,
> Nothing exists in the world but you.
> Search within yourself for what you desire: it is you.[24]

This is how one of my students described his quest for vision:

> The place I selected is on the top of a hill, a fantastic location to sit and think, and I started to slow down to the heartbeat of the planet. The feeling that remains with me now is my connection to the earth.
>
> Being still and watching the sun set in the west and knowing that I was going to see it rise in the east, I could feel the earth turning in space, with me on my hill. The feelings of connection became very strong, and I could see just how affected by the elements we are—the pull of the moon, the sunlight on our bodies, the rain and clouds, everything.
>
> It was amazing for someone who lives in a society that operates twenty-four hours a day with no changing seasonally or with nature anymore, removing ourselves further and further from the natural ways. I have taken that lesson with me. I also got some messages from the wildlife around me that confirmed my questions that I came out with, and when I came down from my hill at the end of the quest, I felt connected once again with the pulse of the planet. It was an amazing experience and very powerful. It still is, two weeks afterwards, as I reflect.

If you wish to try this for yourself, begin with a question in mind—something you will allow the soul of nature to clarify for you. Then commit to a time and place where you will undertake a vigil to find the answers you seek. Don't take anything with you that might distract you. Instead, pay careful attention to nature and your own internal processes as you sit quietly with an empty, open, and receptive heart.

When you feel it is time to go, clear your space, leaving it exactly as you found it, before you return to your home.

Reflect on the information you have received and watch your dreams. What have you learned from your quest, and how does your soul feel now?

The Burial Ceremony

> Inside this new love, die.
> Your way begins on the other side …
> Take an axe to the prison wall.
> Escape.[25]

Like the Sufi practice that Syed Ahsan writes of in his introduction, where the seeker after love remains in a dark meditation cell for forty days, another shamanic method using sensory deprivation to guide and heal the soul is the burial ceremony. In it, the person is buried in the ground or secluded in a cave to experience the enlightenment brought by solitude, darkness, and the healing embrace of the earth.

A hole is dug. The initiate literally digs his own grave so he can reflect, as he does so, on matters of mortality, keeping death as his advisor; and then he enters it. The mouth of the grave is covered with branches and ferns, and the soil is placed on top. Now the initiate lies in darkness, some three feet or so underground, and will stay there for a period of time in his solitary quest for vision, held in the womb of the earth. The length of time varies. For a burial such as this, perhaps a single night is all. On the other hand, the Kogi Indians of Sierra Nevada take their shamans-to-be at the moment of their births and seclude them in dark caves for a period of nineteen years.[26]

There is no need to undergo a physical burial in order to remove yourself from the world, however. Instead, you can set aside a period of 12–24 hours during which you will have no contact with the outside world at all and during which you go on a "dark retreat." Simply lie still in the silent darkness and feel what it's like not to exist any-more. Let your mind go into shutdown mode—and be quiet.

> Quietness is the surest sign that you've died.
> Your old life was a frantic running from silence.
> The speechless full moon comes out now. [27]

During this time, meditate on your mortality in a gentle, not morbid, way. Simply be aware that one day this silence is all you will have. You have a choice in how to live before that day comes.

When your time of reflection is over, open your windows and doors to let the world back in, and go barefoot outside. Engage all your senses, one at a time. Taste the air; listen to the birdsong; breathe in the sky; feel the grass beneath you; take in the brightness and vibrancy of the flowers and plants around you: "walk out like someone suddenly born into color."[28] This is how it is to be alive.

Of Earth and Sky

The soul of nature, and the earth itself, represents the strong core around which the drifting confusions of life can spin but never penetrate our balance and awareness of a deeper connection to the world. The earth endures and its spirit lives on, allowing us to take sustenance from it always. Another way of drawing energy to yourself, therefore, is simply to take off your shoes and go outside on a sunny day.

Connect with the earth through your feet. Closing your eyes and breathing into your belly, imagine roots growing from your feet and fingers, pushing down until they reach the core: the heart of the earth. Let the energy of the center move through you like life-giving sap.

Connect with the sky through your hands. Raise your arms and draw down power from the sun, letting its warmth invigorate your soul. And connect with yourself through your heart. Shout to the heavens: "I am!"

You stand at the center of two immense energies, which flow through you as their point of collection, connection, and transformation. Feel them move through you, and allow your mind to relax, as if in meditation, so no labels are applied and no judgements are made about this feeling. Simply experience love and warmth.

> Be without sensations, without ears, without thought,
> In order to hear God's call: "Come back."[29]

Decide how you will use this energy, and employ it with love, compassion, and good intentions to achieve what you will.

The Compassionate Soul

> Pain will arise from looking within
> And the pain will remove the veil of self-conceit.
> Until the mother faces the pain of child-birth
> The child cannot be born.[30]

In Sufism, there is a spiritual practice which is a meditation on suffering to help us deal with the sadness of the world and the sorrows we hold within by releasing old fears and opening our hearts to love, so we can be truly present and compassionate in our lives.

Close your eyes and bring to mind any suffering you have. Feel it in your body and breathe into the place of your pain. As you inhale, see your attachments to that suffering being drawn into your body, like strands of light, so they fill you completely, and you can see, feel, taste, smell, and hear them fully, in all their glorious pain.

Expand your awareness, breathing in the suffering of every person in the world who shares the same pain as you, until you feel yourself filled with sorrow.

Now breathe out compassion—for yourself and all those who suffer with you—until it fills and overflows from you as a stream of light and love, from your heart to theirs.

In this world right now, at this very second, there may be a million people crying, lost to God in pain, separation, or the illusion of a life without kindness. Such realizations teach us essential truths: that we are not alone; that although our suffering is our own, we are not unique; and that we are all one—all expressions of the mysterious love that is this universe. At this moment, too, a million people may be praying for you, taking part in a meditation like this to transform your pain and offer you blessings in its place.

Breathing in and out, transmute the energy of pain into love, so your tears of sadness become a flood of kindness toward all those—including yourself—who need your understanding in this sad and beautiful world.

Relating to Fatigue

Sometimes fatigue is symptomatic of something deeper that is affecting us: an energetic pattern in our lives that has led to what shamanic traditions call soul loss, where we lose some of the vital energy that makes us who we are.

When the Lover is at one with the Beloved and in harmony with the ebbs and flows of the universe, it is not possible for energy to leak away because he is investing himself naturally, wholly—and only—in truth and authenticity. He is just being himself, instead of pretending to be something he is not and playing games with himself and others.

When we stray from the truth and are out of balance, however, we make ourselves available to all manner of disturbances, leading to weakness, fatigue, and depression. In pain, our souls take flight and must be guided back to us so we are reunited with our fragments and can see ourselves again as aspects of God, shining in our power.

To call back our souls, we must first refuse to conspire with our conditioned minds, which tell us we have lost something and if only it was returned, all things would be well. To conspire with this state would be to give more power away by agreeing that something has gone from us which might never be returned, and that we are weak individuals as a consequence. The truth, when seen through the eyes of the Beloved, is that we are as perfect and as powerful as we can be in this moment.

This is not to say that things could not be even more perfect! It is a reminder only to avoid the embrace of negativity, which is a soul thief in itself. Instead, we must take responsibility for ourselves and do what is necessary to make things more perfect still.

In traditional systems of healing, it is believed that illness and fatigue, no matter what personal or specific form they take, arise because primal relationships with the earth have been broken. We have allowed ourselves to become separate, lost, and out of resonance with the intentions and flow of the universe. The earth is what we know; it is our first love, and healing comes from reconnecting with the natural world, which is the soul of the earth.

One of the simplest things you can therefore do whenever you feel that your soul needs to be recharged and restored is to take yourself to a place in nature where you feel connected to the earth, and which has a sense of stillness and calm about it, then sit down, close your eyes, and simply relax. Breathe deeply and calmly, and let go.

Whatever blockage is between you and the love of the universe, expressing itself as fatigue or a loss of soul, it has a form in the world that represents a separation of some kind. It could be the break-up of a relationship, an illness, or the loss of a job. All these are ways of relating to the form that it takes, but always it was energy before it became a physical presence.

What is the thing that represents separation for you and takes you out of the flow? Whatever it is, hold it in mind and let an image form of the energy or essence it had before it became a material concern. See this as your fatigue, not an enemy here to hurt you, but a friend to give you advice for the perfection of your soul. Talk to this image-being. What is the message it wants you to hear? Can you accept this as your perfection: that things are as they are? What can you do to make things more perfect still? Ask as many questions as you need to, and listen to the advice of this friend.

Breathe in the energy of this friend, and with your out-breath release to the universe the sadness you feel in your soul. Open your eyes, and remember your power and potential for change.

six

The Medicine Wheel of Relationships

Balancing Ourselves & Finding Our Way to the Center

First there's dying, then union

like gnats inside the wind.

RUMI[1]

We have made a journey from birth (the east of the medicine wheel), a time when all that we knew of life was love, through young adulthood—the beginnings of a more self-aware form of love and understanding of the world (the south), through the middle age / mid-stage in our adventure of the soul (the west), to "old age" and the arisings of fatigue in the north.

We have looked at some of the issues and challenges that might occupy us on our journeys to authentic love: the experience of fear (the beginnings of our journey in the east) and how this may affect our understanding of what genuine love might mean; our search for authentic power (the south) and how our ability to use it skillfully might mean the capacity for true love; the possibility of confusion in our relationships and in life (the west), and our need for clarity and vision; and the evolution of our loving selves through compassionate service to others (the north).

On this journey, we have also traced our development from the birth myths that shape us, through the life stories that arise, and the games that we play in consequence of our myths and dramas, to a place, finally, where we can recognize ourselves in others and, through our intentions to heal, bring ourselves into a more balanced relationship with our soul community. The circle is almost complete.

These four directions we have navigated also relate to our souls. *Maqam an-Nafs* (in the east of the wheel) represents learning through our physical bodies; *maqam-al-Qalb* (in the south) represents learning through our emotions; *maqam-ar-Ruh* (in the west) is the use of the skillful mind; and *maqam-as-Sirr* (in the north) is the station of divine secrets and the place of the compassionate spirit. Body, emotions, mind, and spirit: these four aspects of our soul are what make us who we are.

Now the aim of the Lover is to stand at the center of the wheel, whole in body, emotions, mind, and spirit, with a life wiped clean of dramas and petty concerns, so he is in balance with the universe, and all four directions are in harmony with one another and with him.

The purpose of our journey at this stage is to take that step into the center: *maqam al-Qurb,* or place of proximity to God, which may then enable us, through our continued practice, to attain the "divine wedding with the Beloved," where we discover love in its blessed fullness and return to God through remembrance of our True Selves.

Balancing the Four Bodies

The Truth is yourself, but not your mere bodily self,
Your real self is higher than "you" and "me."
This visible "you" which you fancy to be yourself
Is limited in place, the real "you" is not limited.[2]

The aim of Lovers is to create harmony and well-being in body, emotions, mind, and spirit, so they are in balance and can stand in closeness to the Beloved as spiritually complete beings, not a "mere bodily self." There are Sufi and shamanic practices that can help with this, involving approaches such as herbalism and breathwork, as well as meditation and the use of the active imagination. Before we consider these, however, we need to know our current state of balance within the four bodies of our physical, emotional, mental, and spiritual selves, which correspond to the east, south, west, and north of the medicine wheel.

Everything in life wants to be a circle, said Black Elk, the holy man of the Oglala Sioux, whose words were recorded by John Neihardt in his book *Black Elk Speaks:*[3]

> "The Power of the World always works in circles, and everything tries to be round … Everything the Power of the World does is done in a circle.
>
> "The sky is round, and I have heard that the earth is round like a ball, and so are all the stars. The wind, in its greatest power, whirls. Birds make their nests in circles, for theirs is the same religion as ours. The sun comes forth and goes down again in a circle. The moon does the same, and both are round. Even the seasons form a great circle in their changing, and always come back again to where they were.
>
> "The life of a man is a circle from childhood to childhood, and so it is in everything where power moves."

This, too, is the law of karma, as it has come to be known—something we see played out countless times in human relationships, where one lover commits a "sin" against the other, only to find that the sin comes round again, and now they fall beneath it. The reason for this is that we cannot sin if we do not have pain and separation in our hearts, so it is our "sins against ourselves"—our refusal to heal our wounds—that we commit over and over, using our lovers as our mirrors. Our lovers may be hurt by our actions, but we are the ones who truly suffer, until our wounds are healed and our pattern—our circle of sin and remorse—is broken.

When our wounds are attended to and our energies are balanced, they too make a circle. Then we are in the flow and synchronized with the energies of the universe, and, since this energy *is* the Beloved, our souls are in health and harmonious union with everything that is.

In order to be "recognized by God" (the condition of *maqam al-Wisal,* where we stand at the center and find God's embrace), we must make circles of ourselves so we are one with the "sacred hoop of life," as Black Elk called the flow of the power in the world.

We can see just how "circular" we are, and where our imbalances lie, by using the medicine wheel below.

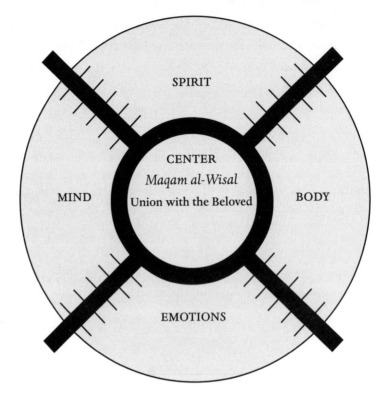

In this simplified wheel, the body, emotions, mind, and spirit are shown.[xv] The central circle represents the state of *maqam al-Wisal*, the place of aspiration for all Lovers on the path, where he becomes the mystic and enters divine union with the Beloved, remembering who he is and his powers as an aspect of God. From this core, four lines radiate out, each marked in five increments. These enable you to draw the map of your soul.

The east, for example, relates to the body. A moment of self-reflection will tell you how in balance your body is. Do you care for it? Do you eat well? Exercise? Get enough sleep? Do you choose your "vices" in moderation? Or do you care little for your body and treat it with disrespect?

---

xv   There are many different medicine wheels, some with the attributes of east, south, west, and north differently arranged. This one is based on the Four Gates model and draws from Native American practices, psychology, and my own experiences with clients and students. You can read more about the Four Gates medicine wheel and its use in therapy, healing, and spiritual development in my book *The Spiritual Practices of the Ninja: Mastering the Four Gates to Freedom* (Destiny Books, 2006).

Our bodies are arguably the most important allies we have on our spiritual paths, because without them we can do nothing. Some spiritual traditions—Western religions in particular, but also those fervent spiritual seekers who are not attached to any particular tradition (as well as those who simply abuse themselves)—care little about the body, considering the spirit and the emotions to be a more pressing concern. But as the psychologist Abraham Maslow pointed out in his concept of the hierarchy of needs,[4] we cannot make progress of any kind if our physical needs are not taken care of first.

After all, how can we create a better world, find and make love, or explore our compassion and divinity if we, ourselves, are starving in a poorhouse? We must put food in our bellies, clothes on our backs, and healing into our bodies before we can give energy to more "lofty" pursuits. When you are too poor to afford a candle, the search for spiritual light and illumination becomes meaningless.

Thus, Rumi, in many of his writings, invites us to view the body as our most important companion on our journeys to the divine:[xvi] "Although the light of the soul is essential, nobody has reached that sky without a body," he writes.[5] And again in these four verses:

> Inside your body is a priceless treasure,
> A gift from the eternally generous One.
> Look for that gift inside you …
>
> I have no idea whether I am a bright soul
> Or a bright body…
>
>
> The body is a device to calculate
> The astronomy of the spirit.
> Look through that astrolabe
>
> And become oceanic…
> The body is a mirror of heaven;
> Its energy makes angels jealous.

---

xvi   Rumi's father, the religious scholar Bahauddin Veled, also pointed to the importance of the body as a tool for spiritual discovery. In the journals he bequeathed to his son, he writes, for example, of *ma'iyya:* that God must be experienced, not just by the spirit, the heart, or the mind, but in every cell of the body if the principle of oneness and the knowledge of our divinity is to be fully understood. See Will Johnson, *Rumi: Gazing at the Beloved,* for further discussion of this.

Be honest with yourself. How do you treat your body? When you tune in to its needs or reflect on your treatment of it, what is it trying to tell you through the way that it feels right now?

When you have an answer, plot the feelings of your body by drawing an arc from the appropriate increment on the line above the word "body" in the medicine wheel on page 130 to the same increment on the line below, as in this example:

The more healthy and in tune with your body you feel, the closer the increment you have chosen will be to the central circle. If your body feels well and good, for example, your arc will be on the line closest to the center. If you feel less in tune with your body, you will have chosen an increment at midpoint. If you are unhappy with your physical self, your arc will be close to the outer circle.

Wherever you place your line is information from your body about the work you need to do in order to feel physically whole. The closer your arc to the inner circle, the less work you may need, as long as you have been honest with yourself.

Now move on and do the same for the emotions, the mind, and the spirit. In each case, tune in to yourself and select the appropriate increment where you will draw your arc of awareness.

You may give yourself a "3," choosing the midpoint, for how you feel about your body, for example; a "1" (closest to the inner circle) if you feel your emotions are well-balanced and wholesome; a "5" for your mind (closest to the outer circle) if your thoughts, suspicions, or jealousies often lead you into unconscious games and actions you regret, instead of being under your skillful control; and a "3" once again for your spirit. If you now connect these arcs and shade in the area you have created, as in the diagram below, you will have a map for your soul at this time.

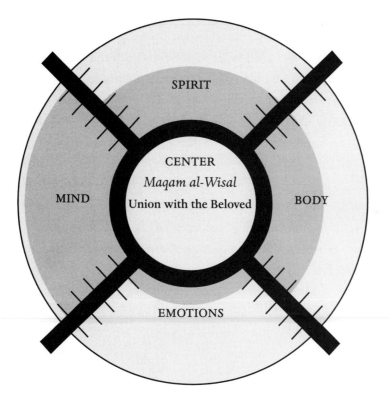

Since all things want to be a circle, which is the universal symbol for balance and harmony, any shape that is not a perfect circle shows you where to concentrate your efforts in order to even things out.

Of course, it is also possible to be a perfect circle, but at "level 5" all the way around. This is useful information too. It shows that you have a certain balance, but that more work needs to be done overall to bring you closer to the inner wheel and your divine spark—to a greater belief in yourself, we might also say. Knowledge is power, because now you know what you need to do and can develop a program for doing so.

If your shape is a perfect circle of consistent 1s all around, of course, then there's nothing more I can teach you—and nothing more you need to learn! For the rest of us, here are some practical techniques we can use to improve and strengthen our souls.

Harmonizing the Physical Self (The East)

> God picks up the reed-flute world and blows.
> Each note is a need coming through one of us.[6]

Plant spirit medicine and herbalism are known to both the Sufi and shamanic traditions. Plants, of course, have medicinal properties, but more than this, they contain a living spirit that is helpful and healing and will work with our bodies to bring equilibrium and well-being. As spiritual beings, the healing intentions of plants are to assist us in whatever way we require it, so we enter through the doorways they provide into greater communion with the soul of the world.

Since the beginning of human experience, plants have played this role in the evolution of our species and the development of loving consciousness. Their form, beauty, enchanting scents, and their healing and spiritual essences have provided access to the divine, and they are still the messengers of divinity, harmony, and beauty. Our souls know plants as friends. We give flowers to people, for example, because they are affirming of love and life and they have a role to play in all of our primal celebrations of life and death—birth and birthdays, marriages and funerals. They are there in the first "I love you," and they are there for our partings too.

Because plants have spirit, the way that they heal goes beyond the administration of a "physical cure" for a "physical illness." Instead they may offer us a new understanding of our lives, a blessing, a change of "luck," a return of vital energy and the removal of negative influences upon us. Through them we may enter new realities to experience a world beyond the physical.

Healing in this way often does not require the ingestion of plants at all but their use in other ways, such as in floral baths, which remove spiritual toxins to restore life and vitality, or aromatherapy, which uses beautiful smells derived from flowers and herbs to bring peace and healing to the body.

According to Sufi legend, the prophet Sulaymān was the first to learn the healing properties of flowers and herbs while he was at prayer one day, and a flower sprang up and greeted him. Sulaymān returned the greeting and asked the flower what it wanted. It replied that it was a healer. Sulaymān noted this and, seeing his interest, other flowers grew around him and told him their healing secrets too, until he knew the cure for all diseases.

Flowers heal, it is said, because they possess *dhat*. This is the spirit of God and the essence of every flower that ever was, is, or can be. Shamans say the same: that every plant is all plants, so that lavender is not just *a* lavender, but *all* lavenders; and since all lavenders are not just a member of their species, but part of the entire plant kingdom, they are not just one flower either, but carry the potency and spirit of all plants.

This shamanic concept also illustrates the magical "Law of Similarity" referred to by Sir James Frazer in his book *The Golden Bough*,[7] which states that "like attracts like." Thus, the effect of a plant is not just limited to its species; if it looks like another plant of a different species, it will act in a similar way, and if it looks like a human body part or organ, that is what it will heal.

Other shamanic concepts in the story of Sulaymān are that plants which grow locally will cure local diseases, and they will tell you what ailments they are used for if you ask them directly. The shamanic practice for doing so is called *journeying*. It is a form of active meditation, as described in chapter 3. Here, you take your attention into your body and allow it to reveal itself as a form of conscious energy or spirit. You can then ask which herbs or plants it most needs in order to heal itself, and how these should be used—as a tea, the ingredient for an herbal bath, or an aromatherapy oil to be used in a burner, for example.

Having identified the herb, you can then look for it in nature or find it at a herbalist's shop and gather a quantity for yourself.

Spend a little time with it when you do, imagining it to be a real spiritual being and entering into dialog with it so you can explore its medicinal qualities. You might then wish to look up this plant in an herbal encyclopedia to cross-check the information you have received with the guidance provided by others who also know this plant. You may be surprised at how accurate you are. But, then again, why should this be so surprising?

At some time in the distant past, before there were "scientists" and "medical procedures," the spirit of the plant must have communicated its purpose to someone in order to be included in an encyclopedia at all.

Two very good plants to begin with, if you wish to restore your body and build your strength, are echinacea and *uña de gato* (cat's claw), both of which are powerful immune system healers. The immune system is what gives the body energy and helps it fight off and prevent disease. These plants should therefore be considered in any regime to empower the body.

In aromatherapy, oil of amber, extracted from the resin of the pine tree *Picea succinifera,* is also recommended as a balancer of the body's energies, and for this reason it is known to Sufis as the King of Scents. A drop of amber applied to the third eye will be absorbed by the body and stimulate the pineal gland, which activates and harmonizes many of the body's functions and leads to increased well-being.

Harmonizing the Emotional Self (The South)

The heart sees the Giver of the secret.[8]

Balanced emotions allow our souls to flower. When we are calm and tranquil, we can moderate the "heat" of our passions to achieve emotional equilibrium. We are then able to avoid the sudden traumas that cause us pain and distract us from the path, so that life's ups and downs have less impact on us.

There are particular herbs that help with this. The shamans of the Amazon use a plant called *chiric sanango,* for example. As well as its physical effects of warming up the body and bringing comfort from the cold, it offers more psychological and emotional healing, also to do with hot and cold, in that it "warms up" a cold heart and "cools" a heart that is inflamed with jealousy or rage. In other words, it helps people open their hearts to love so they discover a more sensitive and compassionate part of themselves.

Chiric sanango can sometimes be found in specialist herbal shops or on the Internet, but failing that, mint can be used instead, as it is also a balancer of the body's physical and emotional heat and promotes the flow of love. For these reasons it is associated with the planet Venus, which was named after the Roman goddess of love.

A good plant to combine with mint is lemon balm, which is famous in Arabian herbal magic for creating feelings of love and wholeness. The chronicler Pliny remarked that its powers of healing were so great that, rubbed on a sword that had inflicted a wound, it would staunch the flow of blood in an injured person without even the need for physical contact. Recent research at Northumbria University in the UK has also proven its beneficial effects in increasing feelings of calm and well-being. It is a great relaxant and a perfect aid to exercises in meditation and forgiveness.

To make a tea of these herbs, simply boil the fresh ingredients (the amounts you use can be much to your own taste, but three heaped teaspoons is about right) in a pint or so of water for a few minutes and then simmer for a further twenty, allowing the water to reduce. Add honey if you wish, then strain and drink when cool.

For a mixture that will last a little longer, add the fresh ingredients to alcohol (rum or vodka is recommended), with honey if you wish, and drink three to five teaspoonfuls a day, morning, noon, and night. These methods of preparation can also be used for the other plants in this section.

Frankincense aromatherapy oil can also be used as an aid to relaxation and for settling the emotions. It is a powerful cleanser of the energies and enhances intuition, awareness, empathy, and compassion. It was, of course, one of the gifts brought by the wise men to the infant Jesus, and it is still used today in religious ceremonies to create feelings of love and harmony among congregation members.

Another means of harmonizing the emotions is the Sufi practice of toning. The long vowel sound *a,* as in the word *father*, will travel from the throat to the heart, where its vibrations can be felt opening our loving consciousness and stimulating our powers of compassion. An alternative, better known today, is the use of the sacred sound *om,* for the same purpose: to bring calm and connection to others and to the divine within and without ourselves.

Harmonizing the Mental Self (The West)

> Intellect deliberates, Intellect reflects
> And meanwhile Love evaporates into the stratosphere.[9]

Plants that work on the mind to enhance our powers of skillful thought are more concerned with the development of nonrational and intuitive information than in the improvement of intellectual reasoning, since our rational and analytic faculties are often what hold us back in our spiritual development. As Rumi tells us, "nothing happens until you quit contriving with your mind."[10]

Intellectual prowess is symptomatic of the "trained" or conditioned mind, which has been taught to behave itself and act in a certain unthinking way. As the word "prowess" implies, there is often also a sense of unwholesome pride or arrogance associated with it, which is a game in itself. To access the greater domains of real genius within us, meanwhile, new ways of thought are necessary, unimpaired by expectations or our desire to be an intellectual, to prove ourselves, or to achieve. In fact, we don't need to prove anything, and there is nothing we must achieve.

Plants that can free us from the shackles of intellectual thought and help develop our powers of insight, clarity, and truth include bracken, jasmine, marigold, mugwort, and poplar. These plants bring the gift of lucid dreaming, a special state of consciousness where we become aware of our dreaming selves and can direct our dreams, which may also be prophetic in nature. The boundary between sleeping and wakefulness becomes fluid, and our dreams are more colorful, richer, and potent than before.

Poplar leaves and buds were a key ingredient in the "flying ointments" of European witches, who used it for astral projection. It (or a combination of poplar and the other plants above) can also be used to make a "dreaming pillow," which will help you to explore new levels of consciousness.

To make one of these, take small handfuls of mugwort and poplar, or some of the other herbs mentioned above, and blend them together. Sprinkle the mix with neroli, orange, or patchouli oils, and bind it together. Then place it in a cloth pouch and put it beneath your pillow. It is said that an intention for dreams based on love is best made on a waxing moon, and dreams about health and well-being are best on a waning moon. Keep a dream journal next to your bed, and as soon as you wake up, note down your dreams and reflections so these messages of your soul are not lost.

Another means of developing powers of skillful thought is to work with plants like valerian and vervain that have psycho-spiritual properties for acuity of mind and that help us to overcome negativity and inertia.

Valerian has been recorded from the sixteenth century as an aid to a restful mind and, in the two world wars, was used to combat anxiety and depression. It is still used for these purposes. It also brings relief from panic attacks and tension headaches, which often arise from an unresolved issue or stress of some kind, sometimes to do with love or the lack of it that we perceive in our lives. By relaxing the mind, the psyche is able to work on the real problem, aided by the plant itself.

One way of taking valerian (which will also aid deep and restful sleep) is by adding equal parts to passionflower leaves and hop flowers and covering them with vodka and honey for a few weeks, after which a few teaspoons of the liqueur are taken at bedtime.

Vervain, meanwhile, was well known to the Druids, who used it to protect against "evil spirits" (nowadays, we might say "inner issues" or "worries"). It will help with anxiety, paranoia, insomnia, and depression. Once again, by relaxing the conscious mind, the unconscious is allowed to work on, and release, our more deep-rooted problems and concerns.

Another plant that protects and eases the mind is garlic. Nicholas Culpepper noted these qualities and wrote of it as a "cure-all." It has long been associated with magical uses, protection from witches, vampires, and evil spells, and Roman soldiers ate it to give themselves courage and overcome their fears before battle. There is also a tradition of placing garlic beneath the pillows of children to protect them while they sleep and defend them from nightmares.

One way to use this plant is to make garlic honey by adding two cloves of peeled garlic to a little honey and crushing them in a mortar, then adding another tablespoon of honey to the mix. This can be drunk in hot water or simply eaten, two teaspoons at a time, morning, noon, and night.

An aromatherapy oil that is good for peace of mind and the expansion of spiritual consciousness is sandalwood, which is especially recommended by Sufis "whenever serious meditation and spiritual practices are being undertaken, because it is quieting to all of the egotisms of the body, especially those relating to sexual energies,"[11] which can often play on the mind.

Finally, there is a toning practice, too, which helps to develop our intuitive mental capacities. This is the use of the vowel sound *i* (as in *regime*), which causes healing vibrations at the third eye, stimulating the pineal gland, strengthening the powers of insight, and relaxing the hold of the conditioned mind.

Harmonizing the Spiritual Self (The North)

In the body of the world, they say there is a soul
And you are that.[12]

Perhaps the greatest plant allies we have for soothing the soul and bringing good fortune and harmony are marigold flowers. Aemilius Macer, as long ago as the thirteenth century, wrote that merely gazing at marigolds will draw "wicked humours out of the head," "comfort the heart," and make "the sight bright and clean."

Shamans grow marigolds near the front door of their houses to absorb negativity from people who pass by. They say that the flowers turn black when this happens, but go back to their normal bright color when this negative energy is dispersed through their roots to the earth. Marigold petals are also scattered beneath the bed, where they will ensure restful sleep and enrich the soul, aiding astral travel, during which we may commune with the infinite and learn its loving and healing secrets. They can also be added to bath water to bring calm to body and soul.

Another practice you might try is to take a bucket of water containing crushed marigold flowers and thoroughly wash the floors of your meditation room, to create a peaceful sanctuary for your soul. You can also drink marigold tea, or eat the petals fresh in salads, to enhance your spiritual powers.

Myrrh is perhaps the most potent aromatic oil to help with spiritual expansion. It is mentioned in the Qur'an for its healing properties and was one of the oils commended by God to Moses. According to Shaykh Hakim, "in ancient times it was used to convey to people a certain internal esoteric teaching, to purify their spiritual environment so that the teachings would have a proper soil in which to be planted,"[13] and it is still used today as one of the most sacred anointing oils.

All aromatherapy oils are simple to use, and myrrh is no different. It can be massaged into the skin, used in a burner, rubbed onto bed sheets for blessings while you sleep, or a few drops can be added to your bath. It is also available in incense form as an aid to meditation.

The vowel sound *u* (as in *you*) can also be used during these meditations. This sound, according to Shaykh Hakim, is "Where our action meets and intermingles with the divine permission, the *idhn*,"[14] and it will unblock (and unlock) the soul through its vibrations, allowing you to connect with the greater soul of the world.

Enhancing Mystical Powers (The Center)

> The real truth of existence is sealed,
> Until after many twists and turns of the road.[15]

When our bodies, emotions, minds, and spirits are harmonious in themselves and in balance with one another, we are better able to find our way to the center—to remember ourselves again and merge with the Beloved. And again, there are practices to help with this.

According to the twelfth-century mystic Abdul-Qadir, who founded the Qadiri Sufi order, the rose is the most magical, potent, and soul-filled of all, and "all dervishes use the rose (*ward*) as an emblem and symbol of the rhyming word *wird* ('concentration-exercises')."[16]

The rose—the Mother of Scents—represents divinity itself. Tradition states that, at the beginning of the world, God created the soul of Prophecy, and that this soul gave birth to the 124,000 Prophets who have since walked the earth. So brightly did the soul of Prophecy shine that it began to perspire, and from the waters of these holy droplets grew the rose.

Every rose, therefore, is infused with divine power and carries the essence of the Prophets themselves. It is for this reason that the rose is considered the greatest ally for mystical experience, the most skillful healer, and the most accomplished teacher of the arts of love (which may be why we still give roses to our lovers today).

Rose water can be used throughout your soul's journey to help you balance any aspect of body, mind, emotions, or spirit, but it is of particular use in helping us attain the mystical state, where the sheets are thrown back to welcome our Beloved.

To make rose water, gather a few ounces of rose petals and place them in a bowl of spring or rain water to soak for at least a day and a night, then decant the liquid into a glass container. This elixir can be used directly on the skin, in bathing water, or drunk; ingestion will absorb the blessing (*baraka*) of the Prophets themselves, and the knowledge of God. Fresh rose petals can also be eaten, used as an ingredient in the dreaming pillows mentioned earlier, or sprinkled onto bed sheets so you sleep among the gods.

Another aspect of Sufi (and shamanic) practice for the experience of mystical states is meditation in dark, secluded cells, as I, and Syed Ahsan, have mentioned before.

The creation myths of all spiritual traditions tell us that there was a time of darkness before the world began, when God was whole and we were a part of that wholeness. The Bible (Genesis I) records, for example, that "in the beginning … the earth was without form and void, and darkness was upon the face of the deep." We find this repeated in the creation stories of the Pima Indians of Arizona, where "in the beginning there was only darkness everywhere," and in many other spiritualities.[17]

Among the Lakota Sioux of North America, darkness is regarded as the home of the spirits, just as it is for the Dagara tribe of Africa, where it is so sacred that light is forbidden when night falls. Within the Shinto tradition of Japan, it is the same, and there is an ascetic discipline called *komori*—seclusion—which is undertaken in the darkness of a cave or a secluded and windowless hut, known as a *komorido*, which is specially prepared and purified so the darkness brings gifts of power and illumination.

And so it is in Sufism. "In the night of this world, when the sun is hidden, he beheld God, and placed his hopes on Him," writes Rumi. In this darkness, "his eyes were anointed with the words, 'We opened thy heart'; he beheld what Gabriel himself had not power to see."[18]

Time spent in darkness is a primal means of reconnecting with our most essential, super-sensual, and mystical states, where we move into harmony with God, Lover, and Beloved as One.

The first step in darkness work, for those who have not tried it before, is simply to experience the dark, though *actively* instead of passively. We have all met the spirit of darkness before, of course, every time we blink or lay down to sleep, but most of us think of these things as interruptions to our normal life—simple biological functions, of no value in themselves—if we think of them at all.

To become a Lover of darkness, spend some time with your eyes closed (fifteen minutes or so at first, building up to longer periods) as you sit in contemplation, and be aware of what thoughts and images start to surface, all of which you might never have noticed before because your attention was so firmly placed on the world out there. How do your taken-for-granted actions feel when you are using other senses to guide you?

Once your competence with darkness has grown, find a place in nature where you can be alone and undisturbed. Put on a blindfold or close your eyes and feel the sun on your face and the earth beneath you. Listen to the wind in the trees. All of these things have a spirit too—the greater soul of the world. The road to our communion is through quiet contemplation of the meanings they reveal; and this, too, is your route to love.

Explorations

The key points of this chapter are that:

1. Balancing body, emotions, mind, and spirit is important for our experience of wholeness, harmony, and divinity, and will enable us to know our true power and discover our capacity for love.

2. We can use the medicine wheel to explore how in balance these aspects are and how aligned they are with each other. Then there are shamanic and Sufi practices we might use to restore equilibrium where this may be required.

Gazing the Beloved

We are, however, more than the sum of our parts. Dividing ourselves into aspects to be worked on, while useful, is also misleading, because it distracts us from the awareness of our unity by suggesting that we can really somehow separate our beings into something other than a single essence.

It is good practice, therefore, to combine any work on the body, mind, spirit, or emotions with another technique called gazing, which is one of unification and will overcome the temptation to regard ourselves as beings who are capable of separation from the divine.

> Behind this world opens an Infinite universe ...
> Everything you see has its roots in the unseen world,
> The forms may change, yet the essence remains the same...
> The source they come from is eternal, growing ... the source is within you.[19]

Gazing is simplicity itself. In fact, so simple is it that Rumi was even at a loss to know what to call it since it seemed such a natural thing to do. "What shall we call this new sort of gazing," he asks, where:

> People sit quietly and pour out their glancing
> Like light, like answering?[20]

In the Sufi practice, taught to Rumi by Shams, two people sit opposite one another and look into each other's eyes, holding the gaze for a period of minutes, hours, even days or weeks. As innocent as it sounds, this was a radical departure from earlier forms of meditation where students would sit facing a wall or with eyes closed so as not to distract themselves from their inner work. This had been Rumi's practice too until Shams shattered his habit by teaching the new technique. When Rumi emerged from his gazing with Shams, it was as if he was a different man and, to his students, it seemed that he had attained a sudden enlightenment.

The practice was no less, in Will Johnson's words, than "a mutual destruction of the limited, autocratic mind, as though a wrecking ball were bouncing back and forth between two buildings and demolishing both of them at the same time. The longer the gaze was held, the more thorough was the demolition of the limited sense of self that believes itself to be something other than God."[21]

By holding the gaze of your lover, eye to eye, even for a short time, physical forms begin to disappear and the face of the person sitting opposite you becomes blurred, ethereal, and then vanishes altogether, leaving a sheen of energy—the true soul—in its place. We are then able to tune in to this soul and see the beauty and truth it contains. With a shock of awareness, we realize that we are this soul too, that we are one and there is a unity behind all things: the essence of the soul we share, which is harmony, beauty, and love.

In fact, it is not even necessary to undertake the practice with a lover in order to gain a sense of this, since all things share the same spirit. Thus, the technique of gazing is also known to shamans who, according to Castaneda, practiced it with plants, animals, trees, and rocks as well. In the shamanic practice, the student sat before a plant and simply stared into it, allowing his eyes to go slightly out of focus and looking beyond the leaves and branches until its essence was revealed as a glow of energy, a life force, or an aura. Malidoma Somé relates a similar exercise among the Dagara tribe of Africa where, as part of their initiation into spiritual awareness, young men would sit before a tree, gazing at it until the spirit it contained stepped out of the leaves and showed itself to them.[22]

Since the purpose of this exercise is to experience the unity of self, even sitting before a mirror and staring into your own eyes will enable you to sense and experience your soul and the wholeness of your being.

As you gaze into the mirror, you will begin to feel a tickling or buzzing sensation in the middle of your forehead, somewhere beneath the skin, as the pineal gland or "third eye" begins to direct your spirit-energy into your reflection. The mirrored surface then beams this energy back to you, and you sense warmth, calm, and connection to your soul-self.

Continue to gaze, and you may find that your reflection starts to dissolve and an aura of light takes shape around the shadow-form that remains, growing brighter in luminosity. Relax into the sensation and understand from this that in reality there is no separation between body, mind, emotions, and spirit; all of it is soul, and your true being is one of energy: the forms may change, yet the essence remains the same.

seven

Completing the Circle

What Our Relationships Teach Us

*A True Human Being is never
what he or She appears to be.
Rub your eyes, and look again.*

RUMI[1]

The center of the wheel is only figuratively the final destination for Lovers, because ultimately the center, the wheel, and the quest itself are illusions. All Lovers (and all people) already stand at the center of their own circles. This is what shamans mean when they say that "the world is as we dream it," and what Rumi means when he relates the words of God to man, that "we are related to one another as iron and magnet. Heaven is man."[2] We are already gods: if we rub our eyes and look again, we can see the truth of this. But that, of course, is also our challenge.

What is required of a seeker after truth is, in fact, not an arduous journey, but a change of mind or perspective, so he sees God within himself and acts in accordance with this. Then he becomes his God-Self, allowing his persona and masks to slip away so the divine can move through him.

"The Beloved has infused all my cells," writes Rumi in the *Ruba'iyat*; "of me only a name remains, all the rest is Him."[3] This is what "self-annihilation," this change in perspective, means.

Our entire reality is, after all, an act of faith, a consensus agreement to see things in a particular way. The Way of the Lover, therefore, is to retrain the mind to see reality differently and for what it truly is: magnificent, beautiful, and already filled with a love we don't have to earn, only live, instead of the way it is normally presented to us—ironically, as something to be fought for.

Rumi labors this point in the *Masnavi* to hammer home his message that "knowledge," as he calls it (or, we might say, *self*-knowledge: our experiences, beliefs, commitments to the world, and our acceptance of responsibility for the actions we take within it) are the most important things we have. These are gifts, not burdens—if we *choose* to see them so.

"The principle of soul is knowledge," he writes. "He who knows most is most full of soul."

> Knowledge is the effect flowing from soul;
> He who has most of it is most god-like.
> Seeing, then, beloved, that knowledge is the mark of the soul,
> He who knows most has the strongest soul.
>
> The world of souls is itself entirely knowledge,
> And he who is void of knowledge is void of soul.
> When knowledge is lacking in a man's nature,
> His soul is like a stone on the plain.[4]

From this we can have no doubt that knowledge of our selves—a change in perspective—is what is most important in the development of love and understanding!

Self-Knowledge: Shrinker of Journeys

The journeys we make in our lives may seem like epic voyages as we undertake them, but in fact, they are only microns: the distance between one neuron firing in the brain and another; a new idea grabbing us instead of a more familiar and less useful one.

Similarly, it may appear that our journeys take a lifetime, but really it is only the time it takes to say, "Aha! Now I see!" The work that we do and the distance we travel, long as it may seem, is all in preparation, so the soil is fertile and the rose can grow.

The realization that love is a change in perspective is available to us all in our personal relationships, which are, in microcosm, a reflection of our journeys to God.

We know from psychologists that successful relationships are based on a willingness to listen, to gain knowledge from each other, to appreciate and to make an effort for new meanings, while those that fail have closed-mindedness and a withdrawal from intimacy at their hearts.

Patience is important too, because it may take time to understand our lovers—for the seeds of the rose to be planted—and we must remain open to the wisdom and insights they bring so that the flower can grow. Even if we cannot fully appreciate these insights at the time, there will come a moment when we do.

There are no accidents, after all. Lovers are drawn to each other for a reason. It may only be so they can play familiar games together, but even then, there is a chance to learn from them.

Then again, once together, a change in perspective may be all it takes for the games to end and real love to grow. Commitment to our lovers, taking responsibility for ourselves, the relationship we are a part of, and faith in the truths of the soul, are what it takes for this shift to happen.

Every relationship—"good" or "bad"—will therefore give us the opportunity for growth and self-understanding. And, since *anything* we do reflects *everything* we do, all relationships can bring us insights into our greater quest for love and tell us how to find our ways not only to worldly happiness but to spiritual peace and reconnection.

The Map of Loving Relationships

Through birth you appeared in this world of the four directions.
It is also through birth that you can escape from your chains …
The birth of the child tears apart the mother's womb.
The birth of man shatters the universe.[5]

Every Relationship Begins with Fear

Fears are the birth pains of love. The medicine wheel teaches that all things are born in the east—with passion, excitement, eagerness, confidence—and with anxiety, too.

This is the condition in which Lovers meet. In the flush of a new relationship, the intoxication of love leaves us swooning. Pleasure hormones—oxytocin and vasopressin—rush through our brains; we become addicted to love and the joy our lovers bring us. The world becomes beautiful, a playground we share together and a place of infinite wonder. It seems strange that only we can see its beauty—and that we never noticed it before! Reflected in the eyes of our lovers, we even love ourselves a little more.

And then comes the fear. We might even say that the fear comes *because* we feel so alive and in love. "What if this person, who is my life, should leave me?" we worry. "What if the spell is broken and my world becomes ordinary again?" "What if I should become who I was before he saw God in my eyes: lost, alone, and unlovable?"

It is at this stage that many relationships fail. After three months or so, our oxytocin levels return to normal and the rational mind, socialized into fear, begins again to control our thoughts. The "what ifs" come to dominate our minds.

With the excitement gone and fear levels rising, many lovers would rather leave each other than follow where their fears are leading: into those dark caverns of the self where they might discover who this person really is that feels so full of fear, what they are afraid of, and why.

This is the Lover's first initiatory challenge: to face her fears and find her answers so she can continue to love with courage. Relationships that make it are between the brave.

For others, love ends and they are back in the game (literally), looking for a new and temporary high to distract them from their suffering and the unconscious fears that drive them.

There is an opportunity for knowledge even in the pain of lost love, because knowing the reasons for our loss can help us avoid these games in future and bring us a love that will last.

"Go, lose everything you have," Rumi tells us; explore your suffering and learn from it. "It is that which is everything."[6] He offers us this caution too: "nobody has ever fled from pain without receiving something worse in exchange."[7]

If love has ended for you, treat your pain as an opportunity, and embrace the wisdom it brings you. Acknowledge it, explore it, and *feel* it. By doing so, you might learn something new: how to love authentically and so find the love you are looking for.

Power Is Only an Issue When We Have Something to Hide

For relationships that continue past the stage of fear, the next challenge, and the next opportunity for knowledge that the universe provides us with, is power, in the south of the wheel.

Every relationship we have involves us in the delicacies of finding a balance of power. Who will lead and find the pathway to love? Which of us will follow? How is this to be negotiated, and what skills do we have that we can put in service of each other?

Authentic power is exercised when we know our truths and do not get caught up in stories—our own or those of our lovers—because then we have no agendas to fulfil, apart from the singular ones of being honest with ourselves and expressing our truths through love. When we allow our stories to hook us, however, the dramas and games take over because they are more exciting than a love that is now past its flush, but which could become even more sustaining to our souls if we allowed it to nurture and feed us.

When inauthentic power guides our relationships, we are always looking for a "win," to prove to ourselves—and everyone—that only we are right. In our self-importance and our fear, we try to make our illusions impregnable, so we do all that we can to make our lovers submit to the views we hold. We become controlling.

Whenever we behave in a controlling manner, we are actually crying for help. We feel so fragile and lacking in real power that we dare not allow ourselves to be challenged or our masks to drop. We want our lovers to rescue us. We hope they will see through our weaknesses without us having to admit it to them, so they are moved to give us the love and guidance we need to become more perfect and trusting souls.

Love asks of us honesty, but even this simple request can be frightening and confusing for some. Our college educations do not stretch to self-examination, and few people know who they really are. Asking them to look at themselves and decide so they can find their truth and honesty is like telling them there are 18,000 different worlds inside them. The message itself is bewildering, and some of these worlds are guarded by dragons and bathed in the shadows of pain, so visiting them at all would be an act of terror. Many are not ready for this.

As an example, a woman once emailed me to ask about a course I was running that she was interested in attending. I replied that she was welcome. I then received a response from her lover, who had intercepted my email and wrote to tell me that his "soulmate," as he called her, was not allowed on this course. I tried to answer his concerns, but when I wrote back, he responded with a further email quoting "research" he'd done on the web that "proved" that the theme of my workshop (freewill and vision) was "dangerous." He even took to phoning journalists to ask their opinion on such courses. And, having taken control of his partner's decisions, he copied every email he sent to me, each filled with his intellectual arguments and hidden (yet so transparent) fears to her.

Unbeknownst to him, meanwhile, his lover was phoning me to apologize for his behavior and ask my advice about his controlling nature. It became clear that this three-way drama was not about the workshop at all, but a battle for power at the heart of their relationship, which was in obvious difficulty. Her lover even threatened to throw her out of the house if she disobeyed him and attended the course—a curious way indeed of behaving toward one's "soulmate."

Shamans call such behavior soul theft: the deliberate attempt to take a person's power by another in order to fill the emptiness and lack of soul in themselves. Usually this results from fear on the part of the soul thief; in this relationship, it was evident that the man was, indeed, terrified. He was afraid of his lover finding freedom because of what she might learn about love, about herself, and about her lover. And he was terrified for himself as well—that his partner would realize that his "love" was really control, then he would have to look at his own dragons and either change his ways or lose his love forever.

I offered the couple counselling, but he had no interest and she was not allowed to attend. I believe they separated a few weeks later—on the face of it, over no more than a workshop.

To be in authentic power, we must be true to ourselves but understand that our *right* to be who we are does not extend to dictating to others who *they* are. Relationships that work do not involve sacrifice, and we do not have to lose ourselves in them.

Instead, they *add* to who we are, making us more powerful, more loved and alive, and provide the mirrors we need so we can learn and grow in knowledge of ourselves.

> After all, what is a mirror for?
> It is to reveal to each one of us who he is and what he is.[8]

Vision Is How We Sustain Ourselves

A commitment point arises in relationships where we must decide to remain with them—that we gain something from their teachings, and they are worthy of the love we invest in them—or that we must leave them, having grown as much as we can from the lover we are with. This is the work of the west: to reflect on the journey we have taken and either see its value to us or find a new path and a vision for the life we want and the love that we have to share.

If we choose to remain, we must be clear with our lovers about what vision we hold and where we want this love to take us (and to be clear on this in ourselves before we even speak). This is simple honesty.

When we share a vision together, our relationship has purpose and meaning; it is going somewhere. On the other hand, many relationships fail because they have no reason to exist. The divorce rate in America is now around 60 percent because we drift into marriages without knowing why or what we want our futures to be.

In fact, even these figures, as depressing as they are, mask a greater sadness. One website states from its research that "the majority of relatively happy marriages are among very religious people, people choosing to live a simple lifestyle, people living in the rural South/Midwest, and recent Hispanic immigrants. If you are a normal American guy, living in a large metropolitan area, marrying a normal college-educated American woman who is looking for the American dream (a nice house, kids, good life), then you have over 95 percent chance of either getting divorced or trapped in a miserable marriage."[9]

This suggests its own reason for relationship failures: that we enter them to act out a fantasy (the American dream) and are, by definition, building an unreal world with an unreal partner, playing an unreal game. When we share a vision, however, which is practical and real (represented in this example by religious beliefs, lifestyle preferences, or a community we are a part of), we are more likely to make our relationships work.

It may be, though, that you find yourselves without a shared vision, and your decision is to move on and leave the relationship behind. The loving response then is to give thanks for all it has taught you and for what, in your soul, it has meant to you.

It may be years before you realize what this was or the value of the knowledge it brought you, but stay open to the possibility that *something* magnificent was created between you, and that your heart and soul, and your capacity for love, have all grown as a consequence of it.

Two years after the end of one relationship, a student of mine had a dream about her ex where she saw him in his house and they sat in the hallway together, not quite knowing why they were there. This was symbolic of their relationship: there had been a great sexual and heart attraction between them, but then their love had just faded away, without even a real goodbye, and surprisingly neither of them really seemed to care. In that sense, it had been puzzling: how two people who loved each other so much could mind so little when they drifted apart.

As they sat there in the hallway, another woman, half-clothed, walked down the stairs and asked the man when he was coming back to bed. She had a look of fear in her eyes, as if she was worried that her man might go back to his old love and she would be left alone.

Suddenly, the purpose of their relationship became clear: they had been together precisely to help each other overcome their own fears of abandonment. They had grown in confidence during their time together, nurtured by each other's love, and when they were ready to move on with courage, their relationship had simply ended, without ceremony or fuss. "And now we are free to help our new lovers get through their fears, because we have faced them together and lived through it," she said.

Leaving a relationship with respect for what it was, and for the lover who shared it with you, is important. By doing so, we take strength from what we experienced, grow from what we learned, and step into a new future with pride at our accomplishments and with our self-esteem intact.

> Be careful not to regret the past.
> Be a Sufi, don't talk of the past.
> You are the son of the moment,
> You are young, you have vanquished time.
> *This* short present moment must not be wasted.[10]

Fatigue Is Our Excuse to Give Up Loving

Fatigue, our challenge in the north of the wheel, most often comes with endings. It is that "is this all it came to?" feeling at the end of an affair, when we find ourselves alone despite the efforts we have made and wonder if love is really worth pursuing.

If we have left our relationship with respect and honored each other for the journey we have made and our loving contributions to each other's progress and the welfare of our souls, then our fatigue will be lessened and we can meet again as "friends"—in Sufi terms, fellow travelers who share the same pathway of the soul and are there to help each other. If we have not, then our suffering may be more intensely felt.

We suffer when we feel that we have failed in some way—that our relationship had some form of outcome that we were trying to get to and have been unable to reach. Such a viewpoint is common—it is the reason why 60 percent of marriages fail: because we enter them hoping for a dream ending, but it is not real. *The journey we are on is the love that we have.* Many people see the outcome—marriage or some other form of "official approval"—as the real love, when it is only the real illusion, because there is no "outcome" to love except to keep loving, whether that love is "approved of" or not.

The aim of the Lover is simply to love—fiercely, passionately, openly, vulnerably, honestly, and unwaveringly—not to look for approvals or outcomes. This begins with loving himself and the life that he is blessed with, not in focusing on "failures" and blaming himself for these. As Rumi reminds us:

> Acceptance is the key to happiness...
> You suppose that you're the trouble,
> But really you're the cure...
> You don't see your own face, your own beauty,
> Yet, no one's face is more beautiful than yours.[11]

Even suffering and fatigue is a form of love, because it gives you a shot at life, knowledge about yourself, insight into what pains you, and where your relationships go wrong. From that you can learn something new and choose a more perfect future where fatigue need never feature.

Explore your fatigue if your relationship has ended, instead of shrinking from it or ignoring it, and hear the message it has for you.

> Don't look for help from someone other than yourself.
> The remedy for your wound is the wound itself.[12]

The Soul of Souls

If you have a hundred doubts of God,
Make them into ninety doubts.
This is the Way.[13]

All Lovers begin their journey looking for happiness. They may find, however, that something else happens as they make their way around the wheel: not only do they learn about love, they begin to see beneath the surface of life and perhaps to touch something bigger: *real love,* the soul of the universe. This is the awareness of another world that we are also a part of, where "what is seen is transient, what is unseen is eternal,"[14] and the wordless knowledge that the essence of this world is love, with no separation or conditions attached.

Once this understanding is reached, the Lover can move inside the circle to take his place at the center; returning, in a sense, to somewhere he never left and to the person he always was before his journey even began, at one with the truth of the world.

Once you forget yourself, God remembers you.
Once you've become His slave, then you are free.[15]

We who are still on the journey can't know much of the center because we have not experienced it. The irony is that we can't know much of it when we get there either, because then we return to the source of all things. There is no separation and therefore no point from which to observe something "other" than what and who we are. The love of the universe flows through us, and the form it takes ceases to be important.

We should therefore, in Rumi's words:

Desire only that of which you have no hope;
Seek only that of which you have no clue.[16]

We get a glimpse of how this must feel when, in our human relationships, we melt into our lovers and forget our "selves" to the moment. Our concerns leave us, our worries and fears dissolve, and we two become One. In that instant, we understand without words or thought that the world means us no harm, that all is energy or spirit, and that we are a part of that energy too—its co-creators, the ones who give form to the world—and that all things are therefore us. I am That: there never was any separation to overcome.

It is then that we become more than "primal Souls [in] the theater of God's court," to use Rumi's words; instead, we understand our magnificence, and merging with the Beloved we become "Soul of Souls, the exhibition of God himself."[17]

No matter how young or old a person is when he realizes these truths, he is always both elder and newborn, a man of knowledge who is also wide-eyed with childish wonder.

Some cultures call such people shamans. They are the "walkers between worlds," connected to the infinite and rooted to the earth. Ego-free, these "Soul of Souls" do not have the same hunger to lead or be "right" as our elected experts—and they are therefore given leadership roles, because their wisdom comes from love and the integrity of their souls.

It is hard, and it can also be lonely for those who stand at the center like this, because our society has no place for Lovers and shamans, and little patience with outsiders of any kind, or their creative and loving inspirations which threaten the status quo. The history of the world is littered with people who were sacrificed by society to maintain its mediocrity, or "re-educated" back into rigid and unloving ways of thought through punishments and sanctions.

The most important thing all Lovers have, therefore, in the face of their loneliness and loving genius, is their unquestioning knowledge of God: their inner certainty of their own divinity, and the voice of their "Soul of Souls" that connects them to the truths of the universe.

If you allow it to, the voice of this soul will speak to you too, from beyond the socialized self, to offer you clarity and love when life throws doubts your way.

Explorations

The exercises that follow let you examine the points in this chapter, which are that:

1. All relationships are, in microcosm, *the* relationship you most strive to have: reconnection with the divine spark within you, and through this a return to the Beloved: oneness, completion, and remembrance of who you are.

2. *Every* relationship follows the same journey as this *one* relationship and brings you to the threshold of a place you never really left: the center, where you can remember. The map for this journey is provided by the medicine wheel, and through it we learn that all relationships begin with fear, move through our

negotiation and recovery of power to the necessity for vision, and, finally, to the need for us to manage fatigue. Knowing the stage we are at with our lovers shows us where we are in relation to the Beloved.

3. When the circle is complete, we have a possibility of stepping into the center: the place of the true soul, the wise elder, and the newborn. A change of perception and a new way of seeing is all it takes for this to happen. Rumi writes of this that:

    > Human beings have three spiritual states. In the first, a person pays no attention whatsoever to God and worships anything—sex, money, rank—but God.
    >   When he starts to learn something deeper, then he will serve no one and nothing but God.
    >   And when he progresses in this state he grows silent; he doesn't claim: "I don't serve God," nor does he boast: "I do serve God"; he has gone beyond these two positions. From such beings, no sound comes into the world.[18]

    The place of laughter and silence is reached when we simply accept that we *are* God.

4. Since we never really left this place (we just got hooked into the games of the world, which distracted us from the truth), we always have our souls to guide us, and as *our souls* are part of *the* Soul of Souls, whenever we explore our spirit, we reconnect with the divine and find answers to the questions we face.

    These final two exercises will help you make that reconnection. They are best done outdoors in nature, in a forest if you can—somewhere you will not be disturbed and which is primal and earthy, so the spirit of the natural world can move through your soul and enrich you.

The Soul of Souls

With your eyes closed, imagine that you have a circle of energy within you that travels up and around your body, touching every cell and every strand of DNA. Let this energy flow for a few minutes and feel this flow of life force and love.

Play with it a little, sending out strands of energy into the world around you. Let it connect with a tree, the grass, the sky, so you sense that these things too are energy and have a spirit of their own, a feeling or a mood that they carry.

Now gather your energy and, in your mind's eye, send it out from your belly, projecting it a few feet in front of you. There (in whatever form it takes), see the image of your Soul of Souls standing before you.

This Soul of Souls has access to all wisdom because it is energy, pure and simple, and it therefore shares an affinity with the energy of all things in this world and the next. Ask any questions of it that you want about the nature of love and truth, and listen to what it tells you about the reality that lies beneath things.

Open your eyes when you are ready and look around you. All things have primal souls and, collectively, a Soul of Souls. Look again at the trees, the grass, the sky, and observe how they glow with light as this soul moves through them all.

> When the attributes of the Eternal shine forth
> The garment of time is burned away.[19]

The Song of Your Soul

Close your eyes and let your breath fill your body. Imagine a cord of energy emerging from your crown and winding up into the sky, then attaching itself to a star which, in turn, sends its energy out to the next star, and that one to the next, until you perceive all the points of light in the universe linked together in one web with you at its center, which is the truth of life.

Feel how your movements, even your breath, cause this web to vibrate and set your own body vibrating with its energy too, as if a string is being played in an orchestra of souls. Allow your body to move to this vibration; spin like a dervish, dance. Capture the sound of this song, too, so you sing in harmony with the symphony of the universe. This is the Song of your Soul.

Without your contribution to this great symphony, the world would be less rich. This is part of the love that you bring. Open your eyes and, if your song has words, remember them and sing them often.

> The lovers come, singing, from the garden, the ones with brilliant eyes.
> The I-don't-want-to-lives are leaving, and the I-want-to-lives are arriving.
> They have gold sewn into their clothes, sewn in for those who have none. [20]

Let others see your gold and hear your song of love.

The Beetle and the Broomstick

ONCE UPON A TIME (which, of course, was really no time at all), a beetle found itself on the handle of a broom, which was lying on a pavement stone. To human eyes, the beetle was an inch above the ground, but in beetle terms, it was a terrifying drop.

Intent on reaching the ground but afraid of the perilous fall, the beetle wandered backwards and forwards along the handle.

Its dismay was palpable. It would come to the end of the handle and try to walk down to the ground, then withdraw because it could not find a foothold. It opened its wings to fly away but then closed them again, worrying that there was not sufficient breeze to carry it. And so it continued its ponderous walk backwards and forwards along the handle.

Things went on this way, in beetle terms, for many days, until it came to the end of the broom again, and this time, so distracted was it by worry and the unfurling and furling of its wings that it forgot where it was and fell off the handle completely, drifting safely to the ground.

Did it then go on its way oblivious? Or did it learn something new from its fall? I cannot say, for I am not a beetle. To my eyes, it was only ever an inch above the ground.

· · ·

eight

Strive to Be a Lover

Throw Away the Books & Start a Revolution!

> *I am ready to show you action;*
>
> *but none will patronize this action,*
>
> *so I present you with—words.*
>
> RUMI[1]

*L*ove is action, not words. It is about going out in the world to experience, to learn, and to express the wisdom of our hearts, so we *remember* ourselves as divine sparks and *apply* our knowledge to the business of love. This cannot be learned from books or poets or philosophers; it is known and understood only where breath meets breath and hearts beat together, because love is to be lived and expressed.

Rumi scholar Will Johnson writes that "lovers live fully in this world. They need not run away from it," and quotes the words of Rumi, that:

> Wherever you are, in whatever circumstances you may be,
> Strive to be a lover …

> May anyone who says, "Save him from love!"
> Have his prayer chased from heaven.[2]

It is the job of the Lover to love, not read books. Rumi said of his writing that he produced it only because people wanted to read it, but it was at best a first step on a spiritual path that must lead to action: we must *be* our love, not lose ourselves in words. At worst, his writing was even a distraction from the truth because, by absorbing themselves in it, people also absorbed his beliefs and did not act to discover life, love, and truth for themselves. So it is with this book.

The most important thing you can do is to *practice love,* because it is better, like the beetle, to feel our fear and take our tumbles—even to make a few mistakes, as all children do—and then pick ourselves up, having learned *something*, so we can apply this knowledge as we continue to love.

This is how all true learning takes place: through experience, not theory. In this way, too, revolutions of the heart can begin and the world can change through our loving actions, whereas time locked in libraries or spent at the feet of gurus changes nothing.

Rumi advised us to forgo the words of others and the definitions they contain, so that we might:

> Know the true definition of yourself.
> That is essential.[3]

And then, not even to get caught up in a single definition of ourselves, but continue to explore and learn and grow:

> When you know your own definition, flee from it
> That you may attain to the One who cannot be defined.[4]

Books are only useful in making a few suggestions and prompting a few ideas, but they are worthless in themselves. You are what is important, because without your song, your soul, and your love, the Beloved weeps at its loss, and all of our journeys are made harder.

Remember, then, that you are God, that the divine is within you, and that the way for others to see this in you and to remember it in themselves is for you to practice your love. Take action. Be a Lover. Start a revolution.

The Wise King

ONCE UPON A TIME (which, of course, was really no time at all), there was a wise king with many sons and daughters at his palace, all of them loved.

With the passing of the years, the wise king grew concerned. He worried that the palace was all his children knew of life, and they would be ill-prepared to rule upon his death. And so one day he gathered his children to him.

"It is time for you to go out into the world and learn from it what you can," he said. "I give each of you my blessings and ask only these things of you in return: that you remember me in your prayers sometimes, and that you come home when the time is right."

And so the sons and daughters of the king left their father and journeyed to the four directions. There they remained for many years, learning new skills, trades, and all the ways of the world.

Some grew rich and famous; others became scholars and priests. Some remembered the king in their prayers; others forgot all about him. Over time, though, they all returned to the palace.

But things were different now. The children, who once had been so close, did not recognize each other anymore. They were dressed differently: some in fine clothes and gold, some in rags. Some wore the glasses and beards of scholars, others had servants to read for them. All of them were altered in some way by the world.

Disharmony followed as the children fought with each other, all wanting to prove that they had made the greatest gains, were most respected in the kingdom, or were more worthy of their father's love because they had made the best fortunes for themselves.

The wise king gathered his children once again.

"My beloved children," he said, "I am proud of all your achievements and efforts in the world, and all of you I love equally. My greatest pride, however, is that you remembered and returned to me when your lessons were learned. Here at this palace, your fame and your riches, your fine clothes and jewels, your scholarship and learning, none of these things of the world mean much. But what you have learned in your souls matters greatly. It is your wisdom and your love that makes you great."

His children began to weep, aware of the distance that had grown between them, and they hugged each other in remembrance of who they were. From that day forward, there was harmony again.

Some years passed, and the wise king died, happy in the knowledge that he would pass his kingdom on to wise and loving children.

. . .

Shhhh.
No more words.
Hear only the voice within.[5]

Now burn this book.

The story of lovers has no end,

so we'll be happy with this, just this:

Goodbye.

RUMI

References and Further Notes

Rumi's principle works are the *Ruba'iyat* (1,600 quatrains), the *Divani-I Shams-I Tabriz* (2,500 mystical odes), and the *Masnavi* (25,700 verses). I have used various translations of these works to avoid relying on only one or two sources. My key reference works are:

- Coleman Barks, *Delicious Laughter: Rambunctious Teaching Stories from the Mathnawi* (Maypop Books, 1990)

- Coleman Barks, *Rumi: Like This* (Maypop Books, 1990)

- Coleman Barks, *The Essential Rumi* (Penguin Books, 1995)

- Kabir Helminski, *The Rumi Collection* (Shambhala Publications, 1998)
- Muriel Maufroy, *Breathing Truth: Quotations from Jalaluddin Rumi* (Sanyar Press, 1997)
- Idries Shah, *The Way of the Sufi* (Octagon Press, 2004)
- E. H. Whinfield, *Teachings of Rumi: The Masnavi* (Octagon Press, 1994)

These are given in shorthand in the notes below, so the references themselves do not become tedious. They are listed as DL (for *Delicious Laughter*), RLT (for *Rumi: Like This*), ER (for *The Essential Rumi*), and so on, the others being TRC, BT, WOS, and TOR, respectively.

Introductory Quotation

TOR, 276

Chapter 1: The Masters of Love

1. ER, 42
2. TOR, 21
3. RLT, 15
4. Deepak Chopra, *A Gift of Love: The Love Poems of Rumi* (Tommy Boy Music, 1998)
5. ER, 106
6. DL, 45
7. Dina Glouberman, *The Joy of Burnout: How the End of the World Can Be a New Beginning* (Inner Ocean Publishing, 2003)
8. DL, 45
9. Shaykh Hakim Moinuddin Chishti, *The Book of Sufi Healing* (Inner Traditions International, 1991)
10. Ibid.
11. Ibid.

12. Ibid.

13. Ross Heaven, *The Spiritual Practices of the Ninja: Mastering the Four Gates to Freedom* (Destiny Books, 2006)

14. *Book of Sufi Healing*

15. RLT, 36

16. Rumi, in *The Sufi Path of Love: The Spiritual Teachings of Rumi* by William C. Chittick (Sate University of New York Press, 1983)

17. Ram Chatlani website: www.toltec.co.uk

18. Colin Wilson, *The Outsider* (Tarcher, 1987)

19. DL, 40

20. Kay Whitaker, *The Reluctant Shaman: A Woman's First Encounters with the Unseen Spirits of the Earth* (HarperSanFrancisco, 1991)

21. Kabir Helminski, *The Knowing Heart: A Sufi Path of Transformation* (Shambhala Publications, 1999)

22. ER, 41

Chapter 2: The Birth of the Lover

1. ER, 2

2. For more on this, see my book *Plant Spirit Shamanism: Traditional Techniques for Healing the Soul* (Destiny Books, 2006)

3. Michio Kaku, *Hyperspace: A Scientific Odyssey Through the 10th Dimension* (Oxford University Press, 1999)

4. See, for example, Sheila Ostrander and Lynn Schroeder, *Psychic Discoveries Behind the Iron Curtain* (Prentice Hall, 1984)

5. See *Plant Spirit Shamanism*

6. Dr. Fred Alan Wolf, *The Dreaming Universe: A Mind-Expanding Journey into the Realm Where Psyche and Physics Meet* (Touchstone, 1995)

7. *Acts*, xvii, 34

8. ER, 136

9. In my book *Darkness Visible: Awakening Spiritual Light Through Darkness Meditation* (Destiny Books, 2005)

10. For more information on this and other near-death experience research, see my book *Spirit in the City: The Search for the Sacred in Everyday Life* (Bantam, 2002)

11. Raymond Moody, *Life After Life: The Investigation of a Phenomenon—Survival of Bodily Death* (HarperSanFrancisco, 2001)

12. In *Spirit in the City*

13. Rumi, in *The Sufi Path of Love: The Spiritual Teachings of Rumi* by William C. Chittick (Sate University of New York Press, 1983)

14. RLT, 25

15. RLT, 24

16. DL, 44

17. David Dobbs, "Mastery of Emotions," *Scientific American Mind,* Volume 17, Number 1 (February / March 2006)

18. Chittick, *The Sufi Path of Love*

19. Marc Siegel, "Can We Cure Fear?" *Scientific American Mind,* Volume 16, Number 1 (December 2005)

20. ER, 13

21. DL, 105

22. Thomas Verny and John Kelly, *The Secret Life of the Unborn Child: A Remarkable and Controversial Look at Life Before Birth* (Time Warner Paperbacks, 2002)

23. Christopher Hansard, *The Tibetan Art of Living* (Hodder Mobius, 2002)

24. Carlos Castaneda, *The Eagle's Gift* (Pocket Books, 1982)

25. Arthur Janov, *The Primal Scream: Primal Therapy—The Cure for Neurosis* (Abacus, 1990)

26. DL, 94

27. DL, 113

28. DL, 113

29. *Book of Sufi Healing*

30. TOR, 22

31. Eric Hoffer, *The Passionate State of Mind* (Buccaneer Books, 1999)

32. *The Tibetan Art of Living*

33. Ram Dass, *Still Here: Embracing Aging, Changing, and Dying* (Riverhead Books, 2000)

34. P. D. Ouspensky, in Colin Wilson, *The Strange Life of P. D. Ouspensky* (Aquarian Press, 1993)

35. RLT, 14

36. *Masnavi*, verses 3591–3634, in DL, 130

37. DL, 132

38. Ibid.

39. Chittick, *The Sufi Path of Love*

40. Marilyn Ferguson, at www.quotationspage.com

41. ER, 52

42. ER, 144

43. DL, 109

44. David Dobbs, "Mastery of Emotions"

45. Adapted by the author from an Amazonian legend related by John Perkins in *The Spirit of the Shuar: Wisdom from the Last Unconquered People of the Amazon* (Destiny Books, 2001)

Chapter 3: Seeking the Beloved

1. ER, 189

2. TOR, 313

3. Jake Horsley, "I Gave Up My £500,000 Inheritance." *The Guardian* newspaper (weekend section, February 25, 2006)

4. Ulrich Kraft, "Unleashing Creativity," *Scientific American Mind,* Volume 16, Number 1 (December 2005)

5. DL, 108

6. Don Miguel Ruiz, *The Four Agreements* (Amber-Allen Publishing, 1997), 34–35.

7. Ibid.

8. Stanley Milgram, *Obedience to Authority* (HarperCollins, 1974)

9. Patrick Obissier, *Biogenealogy: Decoding the Psychic Roots of Illness—Freedom from the Ancestral Origins of Disease* (Healing Arts Press, 2005)

10. DL, 127

11. ER, 146

12. TOR, 49

13. ER, 52

14. Idries Shah, *The Way of the Sufi* (Octagon Press, 2004)

15. *Masnavi,* verses 1366–67, in *The Knowing Heart*

16. ER, 168

17. TOR, 23

18. ER, 168

19. ER, 168

20. DL, 31

21. TOR, 224

22. DL

23. TOR, 150

24. DL

25. Rumi, in Chittick, *The Sufi Path of Love*

26. DL

27. DL

28. This story is an adaptation by the author of a supposedly true event related by Dr. Michael Harner, an anthropologist who was conducting field research at the village when it happened. Harner watched the holy man perform this healing, raising a man from the dead through the power of faith—either that or it's just a good story!

Chapter 4: Life Games and Their Players

1. WOS, 106

2. WOS, 94

3. Eric Berne, MD, *Games People Play: The Psychology of Human Relationships* (Penguin Books, 1968)

4. TOR, 103

5. WOS, 149

6. WOS, 117

7. DL

8. DL, 101

9. ER, 114

10. ER, 73

11. Running alongside these personal games and the fields on which we meet, there are, of course, social, cultural, and institutional games also playing out, which predispose us to behave in certain ways. You can probably think of

many yourself, but two familiar games in Western culture are Girls Are Frail, and Men Are Monsters, which sum up the ways in which the sexes are still viewed by our society and which often lead to injustice for both. Women have had to fight for the right to vote, for example, while men are still drafted to die in wars and women have the choice to stay home because they are "the weaker sex" (and therefore not much use in battle). Two examples of how these social games play out are The Courtroom Drama and The Fourth Estate.

Anyone who has been involved in a court case knows that the legal system is not really interested in the truth or even, in many cases, the evidence itself; what it wants is a good story, and the person most likely to win, therefore, is the person, right or wrong, who can create the most drama. In one child custody dispute, for example, a woman claimed in her written statement that her ex-partner had perilously held a child out of an upstairs window and he was therefore a dangerous and unstable character who couldn't be trusted with children. On cross-examination, however (even before being shown a photograph which proved that her story was physically impossible), the woman changed her evidence and related how her ex-partner had, in fact, climbed out of the window onto a roof to rescue the child who was stuck there—which is exactly what he had said all along. Despite her sudden remembrance of the facts (for example, that there was a roof outside the upstairs window), or her ex-partner's consistent story, which she now agreed with, or the photographs which proved it was impossible to hold a child out of this window anyway because it opened onto a roof, the judge decided he "preferred" drama to fact and inconsistent testimony. Girls Are Frail and Men Are Monsters, after all—despite inconvenient evidence to the contrary. As Rumi writes in the *Diwan* (quoted by Idries Shah in *Learning How To Learn: Psychology and Spirituality in the Sufi Way*, Penguin Books, 1983):

> The Man of God is a wise one by means of Truth:
> The Man of God is no lawyer from a book

A similar game is played by our media, the Fourth Estate, who will periodically report cases of domestic abuse, the underlying myth being that men are violent aggressors, and women are at their mercy. A look at the ManKind Initiative website (www.mankind.org.uk) tells a different story. The ManKind Initiative is an organization set up to support male survivors of domestic abuse. In a recent survey of 100 victims of such violence, it found that 75 percent of men were assaulted by their wives at least once a month; that 33 percent had been kicked in the genitals; 16 percent had been burnt or scalded; and 50 percent threatened with a weapon. Despite this, if they reported the attack to the police, 21 percent of the men were arrested, even though they were the victims, and 47 percent were threatened with arrest. Of the just 3 percent of female assailants who were arrested and subsequently charged, not one was convicted, despite the serious injuries some of their victims had suffered. It is the myths and the games that fascinate us, very rarely the facts, which is why Nasir-i-Khusru (quoted by Idries Shah, ibid.) advises us to:

> Seek the meaning from the Outward…
> Don't be like an ass, content with noise.

In other words: follow your own truth and find knowledge for yourself from experience, instead of buying into stories and noise.

(See www.mankind.org.uk/domabus.htm for further information on the survey quoted here, which was conducted by Dewar Research. Their report, *Male Domestic Violence Victims Survey*, can also be found on the Dewar Research website at www.dewar4research.org.)

12. DL

13. Adapted by the author from a story told by Priscilla Cogan in *Winona's Web* (HarperCollins, 1996)

14. TOR, 166

15. TOR, 200–201

16. DL, 121

17. Ibid.

18. DL

19. DL

20. DL

21. TOR, 106

22. WOS, 149

Chapter 5: Staying Awake on the Path

1. ER, 36

2. WOS, 105

3. WOS, 97

4. TOR, 23

5. In Viktor Frankl, *Man's Search for Meaning* (Rider, 2004)

6. WOS, 103

7. WOS, 92

8. ER, 138

9. ER, 3

10. WOS, 109

11. WOS, 55

12. WOS, 95

13. *The Joy of Burnout*

14. All quotations from Archbishop Tutu are from "Reflections of the Divine" by Michael Bond, *New Scientist,* Volume 190, Number 2459 (April 29, 2006)

15. Alison George, "Will You Still Be Sending Me A Valentine?" *New Scientist,* Volume 190, Number 2459 (April 29, 2006)

16. DL, 83

17. ER, 24

18. Carlos Castaneda, *The Teachings of Don Juan: A Yaqui Way of Knowledge* (Penguin Arkana, 1990)

19. *The Spiritual Practices of the Ninja*

20. *Masnavi*, Story XVIII, in *The Teachings of Rumi*, 165

21. *The Teachings of Don Juan*

22. DL, 18

23. DL, 18

24. BT, 32

25. ER, 22

26. For further information on burial and other practices that use darkness and seclusion as a means for awakening spiritual light, see my book *Darkness Visible*

27. ER, 22

28. ER, 22

29. BT, 52

30. TRC, 172

Chapter 6: The Medicine Wheel of Relationships

1. ER, 125

2. TOR, 317

3. John G. Neihardt, *Black Elk Speaks: Being the Life Story of a Holy Man of the Oglala Sioux* (University of Nebraska Press, 1989)

4. See my book *Vodou Shaman: The Haitian Way of Healing and Power* (Destiny Books, 2003) for a fuller discussion of the Hierarchy of Needs and how it relates to spiritual practice

5. This quotation and the ones that follow are from Will Johnson, *Rumi: Gazing at the Beloved: The Radical Practice of Beholding the Divine* (Inner Traditions International, 2003): pages 52, 56, 58, 59, and 67

6. ER, 103

7. James George Frazer, *The Golden Bough* (Touchstone, 1995)

8. TOR, 22

9. TRC, 156

10. DL, 55

11. *The Book of Sufi Healing*

12. ER, 37

13. *The Book of Sufi Healing*

14. Ibid.

15. DL, 11

16. WOS, 126

17. See my book *Darkness Visible* for more information on these

18. Idries Shah in *Learning How To Learn: Psychology and Spirituality in the Sufi Way* (Penguin Books, 1983), 223

19. Will Johnson, *Rumi: Gazing at the Beloved: The Spiritual Practice of Beholding the Divine* (Inner Traditions International, 2003), 34, 35

20. Ibid., 30

21. Ibid., 31

22. Malidoma Patrice Somé, *Of Water and the Spirit: Ritual, Magic, and Initiation in the Life of an African Shaman* (Penguin Books, 1995)

Chapter 7: Completing the Circle

1. TOR, 311

2. DL, 65

3. TOR, 161

4. BT, 270

5. TOR, 277–278

6. BT, 172

7. BT, 257

8. BT, 166

9. www.nomarriage.com

10. Will Johnson, ibid., 79, 80

11. BT, 81

12. BT, 57

13. TRC, 95

14. St. Paul, Corinthians 4, verses 16–54

15. BT, 5

16. TRC, 49

17. TOR, 278

18. TRC, 68. This translation is by Andrew Harvey

19. TRC, 85. This translation is by Kabir Helminski and Camile Helminski

20. TRC, 60. This translation is by Robert Bly

Chapter 8: Strive to Be a Lover

1. WOS, 109

2. Will Johnson, ibid., 45, 50

3. TRC, 194

4. TRC, 194

5. Will Johnson, ibid., 204

End Quotation

RLT, 32

Index of Terms

action, 4, 24, 26–27, 39, 45, 47–48, 50–51, 66–69, 75, 77, 80–81, 86, 88,
    102–104, 109, 115–117, 129, 133, 140, 142, 148, 161–162
adulthood, 16, 20, 127
Altered States (film), 1
anger, 39, 49, 69, 79, 90, 99
annihilation, xi, 24
As You Like It (play), 86
Beloved, the, xi–xii, 2–3, 5, 7, 9–13, 17, 42–43, 57–58, 71, 76, 113, 120,
    124, 128–130, 132–133, 141, 143, 148, 157–158, 162, 172, 177–178
birth, 2, 29, 34, 43–44, 94, 127–128, 134, 141, 150, 169–170

bliss-energy, 17, 30, 58

body, xii, 2, 9, 15–16, 31–32, 36, 38–39, 43, 47, 51–52, 54–55, 64, 69, 79, 87, 92, 95, 102, 116–117, 123, 128, 130–133, 135–136, 139–141, 143, 145, 158–159

burial ceremony, 121

Cartesian dualism, 31

change, 8, 14, 23, 42, 44, 47, 49–50, 52, 65, 67–68, 71–72, 74, 81–82, 89, 96, 99–101, 113–114, 117, 125, 134, 143, 145, 147–149, 152, 158, 162

circle, the, 128, 147, 156, 158, 178

compassion, 16, 36–37, 46, 49, 68, 80, 90, 98–99, 102, 104, 106, 113–114, 116–117, 119–120, 123, 131, 137

conception, 43

consciousness, the flow of, 41

controlled folly, 118

darkness, 3, 56, 95, 122, 142, 170, 177–178

death, 8, 14, 35, 49, 53, 63, 115–117, 122, 134, 163, 170

death as an advisor, 116–117, 122

dhat, 135

Divani-I Shams-I Tabriz (book), 10, 167

dramas, life, 81–82, 119, 128

east (medicine wheel), 12, 19, 29, 50, 51, 127, 129, 134

ego, xi, 16, 30, 42, 114

emotions, 16, 20, 37, 43, 47, 63–65, 68, 77, 80, 94, 101, 103–104, 110, 128–133, 136–137, 141, 143, 145, 170–171

energy, x, 3, 7, 15, 20, 30–33, 35, 37–38, 40–41, 43–44, 47, 50–54, 57–58, 62, 65, 80–83, 99, 102, 106–108, 116–117, 119–120, 122–125, 129, 131, 134–136, 140, 144–145, 156, 158–159

enlightenment, 9, 11, 18, 26, 122, 144

fakir, xiii, 8

fana, xi, 9, 24

fatigue, 20, 106–109, 111, 113, 115–117, 119–120, 124–125, 127, 155, 158

fear, 2, 12, 20, 24, 26, 28–30, 38–50, 53–58, 62, 71, 73, 75, 85, 89, 107, 115, 117, 123, 127, 139, 150–152, 154, 156–157, 162, 170

flowers, 6, 8, 11, 15, 18, 69, 122, 134–136, 139–140, 149

fly agaric, 1

four bodies, 47, 128–129

four directions, x, 7, 12, 128, 150, 163

friend, the, 54

friends, in Sufi terms, 120, 155

games, 17, 44, 65–66, 68, 74, 78–80, 85–94, 98–103, 105, 109, 114–115, 124, 128, 133, 138, 149–151, 153, 158, 173–175

Games Theory, 87

gazing, 52, 140, 143–144, 177–178

guilt, 3, 39, 66, 116

habit(s), 12, 38, 43, 47, 61–62, 66–68, 96, 100–101, 117, 144

healing, xiii, 24, 38, 40, 46, 67–69, 111, 122, 124–125, 131, 134–137, 139–140, 168–169, 171–173, 177–178

heaven, x, xiii, 35, 58, 107, 131, 147, 162, 169

herbalism, 128, 134

Hierarchy of Needs, 131, 177

illusion, 12, 14, 25, 35, 38, 45, 50, 59, 67, 70–71, 76, 89, 98–99, 110–111, 118, 124, 155

intellectual/ism/ization, 51, 137–138, 152

intention, 47, 54, 66–67, 102, 116–118, 138

karma, 129

keeper(s), 23–25, 36–37, 44

King of Scents, 136

Kirlian photography, 32

knowledge, 11, 15, 18, 23–24, 29, 36, 41, 46, 51, 55, 73, 89, 95, 110, 115, 120, 134, 141, 148–151, 153–157, 161–162, 164, 175–176 life games, 85, 87, 100, 103, 173

life scripts, 62, 65–66

life stories, 65, 70, 87, 89, 99, 128

love, meaning of, 2–3

mantra(s), 54

marriage, 10, 13–14, 32, 52, 78, 89, 91, 93, 153, 155

maqam, 16–18, 20, 30, 42, 85, 128–130, 132–133

maqam-al-Qalb, 16, 20, 57, 85, 128

maqam al-Qurb, 17, 20, 128

maqam-ar-Ruh, 16, 20, 85, 128

maqam-as-Sirr, 17, 20, 105, 128

maqam al-Wisal, 17, 20, 129–130, 132–133

maqam an-Nafs, 16, 18, 20, 30, 42, 85, 128

maqamat, 16

Masnavi, 10, 51, 89, 148, 167–168, 171–172, 177

medicine wheel, 7, 12, 15–18, 20, 22, 26, 29, 50–51, 57, 61, 85, 94, 105,
    108, 127, 129, 132, 143, 150, 157, 177

meditation, active, 6, 66, 135

middle age, 19–20, 127

mind, ix, xii, 8–9, 31, 34, 41, 45, 47, 53, 55, 63, 66, 70, 75, 81, 83, 94,
    101–102, 104, 120–123, 125, 128, 130, 132–133, 137–139, 141, 143–145,
    147–148, 150, 154, 159, 170–172

mood of the world, the, 41, 44, 59

mortality, 116, 122

Mother of Scents, 141

muraqaba (meditation), 6

murshid, xii

mythology, 30, 32

myths, 3–4, 13, 34, 40, 44, 46, 58, 62, 66, 71–73, 81–82, 84, 86, 94, 99–100, 105, 128, 142, 175

  creation, 34, 142

  of the self, 103

  parental, 62

nafas, 47

nafsi kull, 16

near-death experiences, 35–37, 170

north (medicine wheel), 14, 19, 105, 108, 127, 129, 140

not-being, 65, 67, 74

not-doing, 66

obedience to authority, 64, 172

old age, 15–16, 19–20, 127

otherworld, 33

outsider, the (book, way of being), 25, 169

patience, 68, 90, 98–99, 102, 104, 106, 117, 149, 157

payoff(s), 83, 86–89, 101

persecutors, 49, 77–79, 81, 87, 113

petty tyrants, 77, 80–81

pir, xii–xiii

plant spirit medicine (book, healing approach), 6, 134

power, xii, 8, 11, 13, 15–16, 20, 24, 26, 30, 37–38, 41, 47, 50, 52–53, 55–70, 73, 75–76, 78–86, 90, 100–101, 107–108, 110, 116, 118, 123–125, 127, 129, 134, 141–143, 151–152, 158, 173, 177

  authentic, 13, 60, 127, 151–152

  inauthentic, 59, 80, 151

  loops, 79–81

projection, 73, 138

qawwali, 6

questions, 27, 53, 57, 63, 67, 72, 74, 83, 104, 120–121, 125, 158–159 relationships, 3, 13, 26, 30, 38, 50, 63, 72–73, 80, 82, 84, 86–87, 89–91, 100, 102, 109, 113–114, 118, 124, 127–129, 147, 149–153, 155–157, 173, 177

rescuers, 76–79

sadness, 49, 67–69, 123–125, 153

salik, 16

science, 30–32, 43–44

self-importance, 76, 94, 119, 151

selfless/ness, 74–76

self-limitation, 47

separation, xi, 2–3, 11, 34–35, 37, 40, 42, 50–51, 54, 67, 76, 78, 93, 99, 107, 113–114, 124–125, 129, 143, 145, 156

shaikh, ix–x, xii

shaman, 1, 15, 23, 26, 32–33, 38, 41, 43, 52, 66, 80, 98, 100, 116, 118, 135–136, 140, 144, 147, 152, 157, 169, 177–178

shame, 3, 39, 49, 68–69, 116

sin, 2, 129

sorrow, 68–69, 109, 111, 123

soul, xi, 2, 4, 7–9, 15–16, 18, 28–33, 37–39, 56, 58–59, 68, 73–74, 82, 89, 93, 95, 101–102, 104, 106–108, 113, 120–125, 127–128, 130–131, 133–134, 138, 140–141, 143–145, 148–149, 152, 154–159, 162, 169

soul loss, 38–39, 89, 124–125

soulmate, 4, 18, 37

soul-purpose, 38, 102

Soul of Souls, 156–159

soul theft, 152

south (medicine wheel), 13, 19, 57, 61, 127, 129, 136

Spirit, xi–xii, 6, 8–10, 14, 16–17, 25, 28, 31–33, 35, 38, 41, 52, 54, 85, 98, 108, 119–120, 122, 128, 130–136, 141–145, 156, 158, 169–171, 178

suffering, x, 20, 38, 49, 78, 106–107, 109–111, 113, 119, 123–124, 150–151, 155

Sufism, x–xi, 5, 7–8, 24, 27, 46, 67, 77, 120, 123, 142

tahweed, 10

toning, 137, 139

Transactional Analysis, 87

True Self, 14

Truth, xii, 3, 5, 8, 10–12, 14–15, 20, 25, 28, 30, 33–34, 38, 41, 43, 45–46, 48, 59, 68–69, 71–73, 77–78, 81, 84–86, 91–92, 95, 98–102, 104, 106, 108, 114, 116, 119, 124, 128, 138, 141, 144, 147, 151, 156, 158–159, 162, 168, 174–175

tyrant(s), 41, 77, 79–82, 87, 102

victim(s), 49, 70, 72, 76–81, 87, 113–114, 175

vision, 1–2, 14, 16, 31, 94, 98, 102, 105, 108, 117–118, 120–122, 128, 152–154, 158

vision quest, 120

vowel sounds, 54

wazifa, 23, 67

west (medicine wheel), 14, 19, 85, 94, 127, 129, 137

Who's Afraid of Virginia Woolf? (play), 78

zikr, 5–6, 78, 92

Index of People and Traditions (by first name)

Abdul-Qadir, 141

Abraham Maslow, 131

Abu-Ishak Chishti, 91

Aemilius Macer, 140

Archbishop Desmond Tutu, 113, 176

Arthur Janov, 45, 171

Bertrand Russell, 46

Black Elk, 129, 177

Buddha, 25

Carl Jung, 41, 46, 56

Carlos Castaneda, 43, 74, 116, 144, 170, 176

Chea Hetaka, 26

Christopher Hansard, 170

Colin Wilson, 25, 169, 171

Dagara Tribe, 142, 144

David Dobbs, 41, 55, 170–171

Deepak Chopra, 8, 168

Dewar Research, 175

Dina Glouberman, 111, 168

Dionysius, 34

Druids, 139

Eddie Jessup, 1–2

Edward Albee, 78

El-Ghazali, 109

Eric Berne, 87, 89–91, 173

Eric Hoffer, 47, 171

Fred Alan Wolf, 33, 169

Gill Hicks, 110–111

Hakim Jami, 86, 106, 109

Henry Ford, 67

Idries Shah, 67, 168, 172, 174–175, 178

International Association for Near-Death Studies, 37

Jake Horsley, 59, 172

Jalaluddin Rumi, 7–8, 168

Jesus, 6, 25, 75, 137

John Gottman, 113

John Kelly, 43, 170

John Neihardt, 129

John Ruskin, 7

Kay Whitaker, 26, 169

Ken Russell, 1

Kogi Indians, 122

Lakota Sioux Indians, 142

Mankind Initiative, 174–175

Marc Siegel, 42, 170

Maria Sabina, 33

Marilyn Ferguson, 53, 171

Melvin Morse, 35

Michael Begg, 35

Michio Kaku, 31, 169

Miyamoto Musashi, 116

Moses, 6, 140

Nicholas Culpepper, 139

Oglala Sioux Indians, 129, 177

Patrick Obissier, 64–65, 172

Pima Indians, 142

Pliny, 136

Ram Chatlani, 23, 169

Ram Dass, 171

Raymond Moody, 36, 170

René Descartes, 31, 98

Saadi, 107

Semyon Kirlian, 32

Shams of Tabriz, 8–10, 24, 28, 144

Shaykh Hakim, 17, 46, 140

Stanley Milgram, 63, 96, 172

Sulaymān, 135

Syed Hamraz Ahsan, ix, xiii, 24, 121, 141

Thomas Verny, 43, 170

Toltec(s), 41, 43, 169

Ulrich Kraft, 61, 172

Valentina Kirlian, 32

Viktor Frankl, 107, 176

William Shakespeare, 86

Disclaimer

he opinions, exercises, and herbal practices described in this book are for interest purposes only, and any application of these teachings is at the reader's own risk.

This, too, is an exercise in self-awareness and personal responsibility.

Free Catalog

Get the latest information on our body, mind, and spirit products! To receive a **free** copy of Llewellyn's consumer catalog, *New Worlds of Mind & Spirit,* simply call 1-877-NEW-WRLD or visit our website at www.llewellyn.com and click on *New Worlds.*

LLEWELLYN ORDERING INFORMATION

Order Online:
Visit our website at www.llewellyn.com, select your books, and order them on our secure server.

Order by Phone:
- Call toll-free within the U.S. at 1-877-NEW-WRLD (1-877-639-9753). Call toll-free within Canada at 1-866-NEW-WRLD (1-866-639-9753)
- We accept VISA, MasterCard, and American Express

Order by Mail:
Send the full price of your order (MN residents add 6.5% sales tax) in U.S. funds, plus postage & handling to:

Llewellyn Worldwide
2143 Wooddale Drive, Dept. 978-0-7387-1117-1
Woodbury, MN 55125-2989

Postage & Handling:

Standard (U.S., Mexico, & Canada). If your order is:
$24.99 and under, add $3.00
$25.00 and over, FREE STANDARD SHIPPING

AK, HI, PR: $15.00 for one book plus $1.00 for each additional book.

International Orders (airmail only):
$16.00 for one book plus $3.00 for each additional book

Orders are processed within 2 business days.
Please allow for normal shipping time. Postage and handling rates subject to change.

Sensual Love Secrets for Couples

The Four Freedoms of Body, Mind, Heart & Soul

AL LINK & PALA COPELAND

Is it possible to stir up passion after the flames of romantic love die down? How can one maintain a loving relationship that satisfies and stimulates year after year?

Sensual Love Secrets for Couples offers one simple solution for stoking the fires of lifelong intimacy: awakening and uniting the Body, Mind, Heart, and Soul. These four freedoms—the essence of human nature—have the power to transform a lusterless partnership into a divine union sparkling with limitless pleasure and unconditional love. Featuring over one hundred exercises and fun activities, this practical guide helps readers explore the physical senses, establish trust, cultivate emotional intimacy, achieve sacred sex, embrace commitment, pledge selfless intentions, and build spiritual bonds to last a lifetime.

0-7387-0965-4, 7½ x 9⅛, 216 PP. $14.95

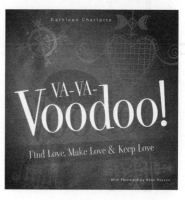

Va-Va-Voodoo!

Find Love, Make Love & Keep Love

KATHLEEN CHARLOTTE

How many professional therapists can put together a powerful mojo bag or an intoxicating love perfume to attract a mate? As a relationship counselor and a Voodoo initiate, Kathleen Charlotte offers the best of both worlds in her refreshing, witty, and magical guide to this crazy little thing called love.

Va-Va-Voodoo introduces five key Voodoo lwa, or "angels," including Baron, the spirit who loves spicy rum and cigars, and La Sirène, an ocean goddess of seduction and sensuality. Readers learn how to "feed the spirits" and request their help in attracting a lover, finding "the one," keeping a relationship steamy, or recovering from heartbreak. A perfect blend of practical magic and inspiring, down-to-earth advice, this one-of-a-kind book includes magic rituals, charms, aphrodisiacs, and spells, as well as helpful relationship tips regarding communication, self-esteem, intimacy, sex, break-ups, and forgiveness.

0-7387-0994-8, 7 X 7, 168 PP. $14.95

To Write to the Author

If you wish to contact the author or would like more information about this book, please write to the author in care of Llewellyn Worldwide and we will forward your request. Both the author and the publisher appreciate hearing from you and learning of your enjoyment of this book and how it has helped you. Llewellyn Worldwide cannot guarantee that every letter written to the author can be answered, but all will be forwarded. Please write to:

Ross Heaven
℅ Llewellyn Worldwide
2143 Wooddale Drive, Dept. 978-0-7387-1117-1
Woodbury, MN 55125-2989

Please enclose a self-addressed stamped envelope for reply,
or $1.00 to cover costs. If outside U.S.A., enclose
international postal reply coupon.

Many of Llewellyn's authors have websites with additional information and resources. For more information, please visit our website:

HTTP://WWW.LLEWELLYN.COM